The
Power of
Kindness
for Teens

Stories Selected by Mary Lou Carney
Editor of *Guideposts for Teens*

Ideals Publications • Nashville, Tennessee

ISBN 0-8249-4630-8

Published by Ideals Publications
A division of Guideposts
535 Metroplex Drive, Suite 250
Nashville, Tennessee 37211
www.idealsbooks.com

Printed and bound in U. S. A.

Library of Congress Cataloging-in-Publication Data

The power of kindness for teens : true stories written by teens for teens
from the pages of Guideposts.
p. cm.
ISBN 0-8249-4630-8 (alk. paper)
1. Kindness. 2. Teenagers—Conduct of life. I. Guideposts Associates.
BJ1533.K5.P69 2004
177'.7'0835—dc22

2004006393

10 9 8 7 6 5 4 3 2 1

Contents

Serving
Others
with
Kindness

Soup Kitchen Seamstress

BY SHIFRA MINCER

It was my first Monday afternoon volunteering at the soup kitchen, which was housed in the basement of Hebrew Union College in New York City. My friend, Rebecca, had begged me to come as part of an after-school service project. I did, but I wasn't crazy about the idea. I was super-shy.

Love and kindness are never wasted. They always make a difference. They bless the one who receives them, and they bless you, the giver.
BARBARA DE ANGELIS

As long as I don't have to talk to people, I'll be fine, I thought, as I delivered plates of stew and rice to a table full of homeless people.

Suddenly someone asked the volunteers, "Does anyone know how to sew?"

I looked around.

"Can anyone here sew?" the man asked louder.

Sewing is in my blood. One of my grandmothers made all her children's clothes by hand. My other grandmother owned a tailor shop. My dad is handy with a needle, and my mom repairs all our clothes and sews curtains for our apartment. I'm no expert, but I can sew a little too. I just hated to stand out in a crowd.

"Um, yeah, I know how to sew," I whispered, raising my hand a little.

My teacher, Ms. Ginsberg, nudged me. "Say it louder!"

I shuffled forward. "I can sew."

The man handed me a box with a few spools of thread, a couple of needles, and some buttons. He directed me toward a chair and table in the hallway where homeless people filed in. Someone announced: "If you need anything sewn, bring it here!" *Oh no,* I thought. *All these scary people will be coming up to me and I'll have to talk to them.* I wanted to crawl in a hole. But I sat down and threaded a needle.

No act of kindness, no matter how small, is ever wasted.
Aesop

"This seam is torn," a man said, poking his finger through a hole in his filthy, tattered jacket. I didn't look up at him as I stitched it. I could only see his worn shoes and the dusty cuffs of his pants.

"Can you sew this button on?" a woman asked, handing me a blouse. *Why do I feel like the whole room is watching me?*

Word soon got around that someone was repairing clothes for free. As I sewed, I could sense people crowding near me; but I stayed focused on my work. I don't know how many holes I stitched, how many bags I mended, how many buttons I replaced before my teachers came to get me.

"Shifra, we have to go now."

I looked up at the disappointed faces of two women still waiting to get their clothes mended. "I'm really sorry, I have to go," I mumbled. "I promise I'll be back next week."

A kind and compassionate act is often its own reward.
William John Bennett

The next Monday, I rode the subway to the shelter. The same thing happened—when time was up I still had more things to sew. So I returned again and again. I felt awkward having to make conversation, but there was so much to be done. *If I don't do this, who will?* I continued going every Monday, even after the teacher stopped bringing kids a couple of months later.

I sewed jackets, pants, shirts, and blouses. I stitched up baseball hats and reattached the sole of a shoe. I mended worn-out bags, taping them together when they were too far gone.

People would try to talk to me, but I'd give one-word answers. I had no idea how to talk with homeless people. They seemed so different from me. Some of them didn't want to leave their prized possession with me while they ate, so they hovered over me while I worked. I felt uncomfortable and rushed.

One day, a neatly dressed woman dragged a chair over next to me. She reminded me more of my grandmother than a homeless person.

"My name's Linda," she told me. "Let me have a needle and thread."

I gave it to her and went back to my sewing.

Linda started sewing her own clothes. After a few minutes, she leaned toward me, squinting. "What're you doing there?" she said.

Wherever there is a human being, there is an opportunity for kindness.
Seneca

"Sewing on a button."

"Hmm. Why are you going from hole to hole randomly?" She took the shirt I was working on and started pulling out my stitching. "You should go through the holes in the same pattern, so your thread makes an eleven," she said as she sewed the button on. I took the shirt back and thanked her. *Maybe I can actually learn something here*, I thought.

A few minutes later a man handed his umbrella to me.

"Can you fix this?" he asked. The fabric flopped freely, unattached to the metal on one side.

"I'm not sure," I mumbled.

Kindness is the golden chain by which society is bound together.
Johann Wolfgang von Goethe

Linda snatched the umbrella. "Of course she can!"

Linda showed me how to make a sheath of fabric to slip over the metal rods. It was pretty cool.

One old man hovered around me almost every time I was there. He had white hair and filmy glasses, and his shabby jacket only half-covered his arms. Every week he called himself by a different name, but he used the name Larry a lot, so that's what everyone called him. Larry came up to me one day.

"You want to marry me?" he said.

I tried to ignore him.

"Run off to Las Vegas with me!" he said.

"I can't go with you, I'm too young," I said, hoping he'd go away.

"We can walk there in five minutes!" he'd say. "Or we can fly! I'll hide you in my bag!"

The security guard came over. "Let me know if Larry makes you uncomfortable," he said. "But don't worry, he's harmless. He doesn't even eat here, he just comes in to talk."

These people need friends as much as they need a seamstress, I thought.

The next summer, I went to camp for three

weeks. I enjoyed myself, but I couldn't help thinking about the people at the soup kitchen. When it rained, I wondered if they were dry. On hot nights, I hoped they'd find somewhere cool to sleep. I was surprised at how much I missed them.

When I returned to the soup kitchen, it was like I was a celebrity.

"Our seamstress is back!"

"Shifra's here! Shifra's here!"

"Sweets for the sweet," said one lady, handing me a candy bar.

We may give without loving, but we cannot love without giving.
BERNARD MELTZER

Linda smiled as she settled into the chair next to me. I was so happy to see everyone—for once I didn't even *mind* being the center of attention.

Before long, Larry shuffled over. "You know who my sweetheart is?" he said to Linda. "You know who I'm going to marry?"

"You get away from her," Linda said.

"It's okay, Linda," I said. "He doesn't mean any harm."

"So how about it?" Larry said.

"Sorry, I can't," I said. "I already have a husband and a thousand grandchildren!" Larry burst out laughing. After we talked a while, he finally wandered away.

I was still smiling when another man walked up.

I'd seen him before, but had never spoken with him. He was small and quiet, and he stared at me without blinking, like an owl. He clutched a shirt to his chest.

"Can I take a look?" I asked softly. I recognized his expression immediately. I knew all about being shy and afraid. But once I had begun helping people, once I started really listening and talking to them, my shyness had melted away.

The man reluctantly handed me his shirt. "The pocket," he mumbled.

It's nice to be important, but it's more important to be nice.
Author Unknown

I eyed the outline of thread where a pocket used to be. Linda peered over my shoulder. "Mmm, tough job," she said.

The shirt was ragged, but I knew I could fix it. Before I was finished, I might even be able to draw this guy into a conversation. "It may take me a while, but I can make a new pocket for you," I said. He looked worried, so I held his shirt out to him. "It's up to you, but I promise I'll be really careful with it."

The man stepped away, paused, then stepped back. "Okay," he said, nervously. "Thank you."

I looked him in the eyes and smiled. "Thank *you*," I said.

Bride for a Day

By Lisa Arrett

I was married on June 22, 2002.

Well, kind of. I wasn't in love with the groom. Actually, we'd never gone on a date.

The truth is, the whole wedding was a fake. It was staged for the residents of Country House in Davenport, Iowa, a home for Alzheimer's patients.

People with Alzheimer's disease live in the moment. They suffer from a brain disorder that affects short-term memory, so most of the time they can't remember what they ate for breakfast or who visited them the day before. But they *can* often remember things that happened long ago, and those memories are comforting to them. They just need something to remind them of those happy times. Something like a wedding.

Kindness: a language the deaf can hear and the blind can see.

Author Unknown

Near the end of my senior year of high school, I worked part-time as a caregiver at Country House. My job was to help make beds for the thirty-two residents, take them to the bathroom, give them showers, and help with meals and activities. I'd only been working at Country House for a few weeks when Judy, the activity director, stopped me in the hall and asked me to be the "pretend" bride.

"You'll get married, open gifts, attend the reception," she said. "I've got a few wedding dresses, and I'm sure one will fit you."

They may forget what you said, but they will never forget how you made them feel.
CARL W. BUECHNER

I pictured myself in a long, flowing gown, walking down the aisle. *What a blast!* But it also felt weird.

"Judy, isn't this kind of dishonest?" I said. "I mean, making the residents think it's a real wedding and all?"

She smiled. "We do it every June, and the residents *love* it. It touches them. You really won't believe it."

Judy was the expert, but I was still skeptical. Sure, it would be fun to dress up. But what would it really *do* for these people? Most of them wouldn't even remember it the next day.

"Okay," I finally agreed. "Who's my groom?"

"I haven't found one yet. Do you know anyone who could do it?"

I decided to ask Ash, a classmate and close friend of mine, to "marry" me. He was really into theater, and he jumped at the chance. I was offically fake-engaged.

The next day at work, Judy brought out three bridal gowns that the owner of a resale shop had donated. They weren't the latest fashion, but they were still beautiful. I stepped into one gorgeous white gown, covered in lace and pearls. "It's perfect!" Judy said. "Go look at yourself. There's a big mirror in the hall."

In the hallway I saw Irene, a resident who walks slowly, with head down and eyes focused on the floor. She hardly ever speaks; but when she noticed me, her eyes lit up and she rushed down the hall.

"Oh my goodness, honey!" she said, fluffing my gown. "Don't you look beautiful? Just beautiful!"

Maybe there really is something to this, I thought. That dress sure sparked something in Irene.

Kindness is more than deeds. It is an attitude, an expression, a look, a touch. It is anything that lifts another person.
C. Neil Strait

The day of the wedding, the large room at Country House was transformed. The staff tied ribbons on chairs and arranged them in rows. They hung white streamers and crepe paper bells from the ceiling. They even collected old wedding photos of the residents and placed them around the room. The scent of fresh flowers and candles filled the air.

On cue, someone started the music. Three bridesmaids, wearing pink gowns with puffy sleeves, walked down the aisle, followed by groomsmen, flower girls, and ringbearers. Everyone in the wedding either worked at Country House or was related to somebody who did.

At last, the wedding march filled the room. I took a deep breath and rearranged my veil. All the residents stood and faced the back of the room, eager to see me.

This feels like a real wedding!

Who is wise and understanding among you? Let him show it by his good life, by deeds done in the humility that comes from wisdom.
James 3:13

As I walked down the aisle, I looked into the faces of the residents. In many of them, I saw emotions I wasn't expecting. Happiness. Joy. Excitement. *Nobody* seemed agitated or upset—the way Alzheimer's patients sometimes are with new experiences.

"Hi, Ada," I whispered when I saw her wiping a tear from her eyes.

I smiled at Cecil as I passed. He stood proudly in his suit, hands folded. I'd seen him earlier helping one of the groomsmen create a perfect knot in his tie.

As I walked by Fern, Esther, and Shirley, I heard

them whispering. "Look at her!" "Beautiful. . . ." "He's so handsome. . . ."

By the time I reached Ash at the front, I realized that this was more than just a pretend wedding. Judy was right. People were touched by this, and that's something that Alzheimer's patients don't feel often enough.

After the wedding ceremony was over, Ash and I cut and served a beautiful three-tiered wedding cake that a grocery store had donated. We even opened gifts—Judy had wrapped up her grandmother's antique china and glassware. Then we danced to songs from the Big Band era.

A kind heart is a fountain of gladness, making everything in its vicinity freshen into smiles.

Washington Irving

As we left the dance floor for the last time, Ada ran over to me.

"Hi, Ada."

"Oh honey, you look so beautiful! Just like my own daughter."

"Thanks, Ada," I said.

As she walked away, I knew that by tomorrow Ada would have forgotten all about this wedding. But for now, she was happy.

Everybody Hates Needles

BY JILL MAXBAUER

Crack. *Snap.* I blew tiny bubbles with my sugar-free gum as I parked my truck in the visitor's lot at the hospital. *Wonder how bad this kid will be?* I'd been volunteering here for four years, but sometimes it seemed like only yesterday that I was rushed to the intensive care unit myself.

I was twelve when I noticed something wrong. That winter, I never seemed to have energy. When I went sledding, I barely had the strength to climb up the hill. I was thirsty all the time too. My gym teacher gave me a hard time because I asked to visit the drinking fountain again and again. By spring, my parents were really concerned about my health.

Be kind, for everyone you meet is fighting a hard battle.

PHILO

"You look so pale and thin," Mom said one night. "I'm taking you to see Dr. Taylor tomorrow."

The first thing Dr. Taylor did was give me a blood test. "Jill, you're *very* sick," he said. "You have diabetes, and you need to go to the emergency room right away."

Diabetes? Me?

That afternoon, I found myself in the hospital's pediatric intesive care unit. Lying there, I felt like a fallen telephone pole with lines coming out of my arms and legs. One machine measured my heart rate. Another dripped insulin into my veins. Yet another fed me saline solution to re-hydrate my body.

That afternoon I learned that I had "Type I," or "Juvenile," diabetes. My pancreas had stopped working, and my body wasn't producing the insulin it needed to process my food into energy. My system was shutting down; only a day or two more and I'd have ended up in a coma.

Kindness is an essential part of God's work and ours here on earth.
Billy Graham

"You'll have to stop eating sugar," the doctor told me. "And you'll have to take shots of insulin to stay alive."

Shots? I didn't want to think about it. Finally, the doctors and nurses left me alone and I closed my eyes, shutting out the noise.

When I woke up, two nurses were in my room.

"Jill, you need to start performing your own shots," one of them said. "You can't leave the hospital until you learn how."

The other nurse handed me a syringe filled with salt water. "We'll watch you practice."

The little needle felt heavy. "Where should I practice?"

"In the side of your stomach."

My stomach!

"It should be a quick jab. Fast and painless."

Painless?

My hands shook as I lowered the needle toward my skin. I couldn't poke myself. Twice I got close and pulled away.

"Maybe if I tried my arm," I pleaded.

"No, it has to be your stomach. That's where the insulin will absorb the quickest into your bloodstream."

Little deeds of kindness, little words of love, Help to make earth happy like the heaven above.

JULIA A. FLETCHER CARNEY

Tears ran down my cheeks.

The first nurse sighed. "Okay, Jill, we'll give you a while to relax."

They left me with the syringe. I held it for over an hour. The thought of pushing the sharp needle into my skin was unbearable. *I'm going to have to do this three times a day, for the rest of my life.*

Again the nurses assembled in my room, and this time my mother came with them. They gathered around my bed. I felt like I was onstage.

"If you can't give yourself a shot," one of the nurses said, "your mother can learn to do it."

"No," I said. "I'll do it."

I'd have to be dependent on insulin. But I wasn't going to be dependent on other people.

I took a deep breath and put the needle to my belly. As I exhaled I slowly slid it into my skin. This time I kept pushing. I didn't jab it in like they told me to. I did it *my* way. With a steady hand, I pressed the plunger.

Life is short. Be swift to love! Make haste to be kind!
Henri F. Amiel

The nurses applauded. "Good job, Sweetie," my mother whispered.

Now, five years later, I was headed down the familiar hallways of the ICU. Only this time I was a volunteer. I'd received a call that morning saying they had a new case of Type I diabetes. An eight-year-old boy with blonde hair sat up in the bed when I entered the room. He wore pajamas that looked like a baseball uniform.

"Hi Simon, I'm Jill. I came to visit you. I have diabetes too." I recognized his scared look. "Do you like baseball?" I asked.

He smiled, but didn't say a word.

"I started playing when I was your age. I'm a catcher. Have you ever been to a Detroit Tigers game?"

"No," he whispered. "But my dad said we could go this year."

"My dad likes baseball too. He once caught a fly ball at a Cubs game!"

"Really? I'd give anything to catch one!" said Simon.

I pulled a chair up to his bed and handed him an orange from my purse. "So I was thinking that maybe I could show you how I do my shots. If you want to, you could practice on that orange."

"Oh . . . okay."

"I was so scared the first time I had to do this," I said as I rolled my sweatshirt up a couple inches. "But people are always afraid of things they've never done before." I pushed the tip of the syringe into my side. "It gets easier each time."

I got another syringe out of my purse and handed it to him. He modeled my performance, piercing the flesh of the orange.

Kindness is the golden key that unlocks the hearts of others.
Henry Drummond

"You're a natural," I beamed.

Simon's glance shifted to his practice syringe resting on the table. I wondered how long he had been staring at it.

"It's up to you. You can try it on yourself if you're ready."

Take it.

He took it.

He held the needle for a few minutes. Then he rolled up his shirt and placed the tip where the nurse had drawn a circle with a blue marker. He closed his eyes.

You can do it, Simon.

He was still, then suddenly he pushed the tip through his skin. When he was done, he blinked a few times and grinned.

Only a life in the service of others is worth living.
Albert Einstein

"You did it, Simon! Excellent technique." I cracked my gum. "Hey, did you know that fans are supposed to give fly balls back at some ballparks?"

"No way!" he said. "Why would you ever give them back?"

I shrugged my shoulders and smiled.

Sometimes giving back feels great.

Mom's Bank

by Jillian Marenda

"Jillian! Don't you dare touch that cake!" I halted, knife in hand. My mother was three rooms away, but her "Mom Radar" couldn't be fooled. With me in the kitchen, her poor chocolate cake didn't have a chance.

Mom joined me in the kitchen. "I want you to take the cake to Mrs. Rose. With her husband in the hospital and her little boy sick with bronchitis, I'm sure baking isn't on her must-do list." Mom motioned to a dress draped over the back of a chair. "And while you're out, can you drop that dress off at Mrs. Darcy's? The poor woman's hands are so crippled by arthritis that she can't sew anymore. I hemmed it for her."

When one begins to purposefully perform acts of kindness, the spirit changes, and soon doing good deeds becomes a focal point for our life.

Gary Ryan Blair

I let out a groan. *Not again.* Behind Mom's back, the neighborhood teens call her Saint Marenda—and that's a criticism, not a compliment. It's one thing to help people every so often, but Mom does it *all* the time. She's always cooking for other families or doing their wash or sewing. She baby-sits. She drives elderly people to their doctors' appointments. She convinces area merchants to donate prizes to senior-citizen events. And she's decided to become the "hand-me-down" expert of the neighbohood. She collects all the clothing kids and adults have outgrown, then passes them on to others.

"It wouldn't hurt you to smile and be nice once in a while," Mom said. "I'm going to start calling you Miss Sour Face."

"It wouldn't hurt you to say *no* to other people once in a while," I replied. "I'm going to start calling you Saint Marenda just like everybody else does."

The minute the words left my lips I was sorry I'd said them. Hurt flashed in my mother's eyes and she looked away. I tried to explain.

Three things in human life are important: the first is to be kind; the second is to be kind; and the third is to be kind.

Henry James

"Look, Mom," I said. "You and Dad are always talking about how we have so many bills to pay, how we have to cut back. You do all this stuff for other people for free. People who are perfectly capable of paying you. Your time is worth money, Mom. At the end of each week you should be making a deposit in the bank instead of ending up with nothing."

Mom sighed. "Honey, doing good deeds for people is better than having money in the bank."

Oh, please, I thought. *This is vintage Saint Marenda.*

"Most people would rather deposit cash than good deeds, Mom. Makes it a lot easier to pay the electric bill."

Mom gave me her whatever-you-say-dear smile as she brushed some stray hairs across my forehead. "Well, you better get going with that cake and dress before it begins to snow. They're predicting a major blizzard tonight."

Do all the good you can. By all the means you can. In all the ways you can. In all the places you can. At all the times you can. To all the people you can. As long as ever you can.
John Wesley

The blizzard tuned out to be a whopper. It dumped two feet of snow on our neighborhood. We had just started to dig out the streets and sidewalks when, a couple days later, another storm added six inches of ice on top of the pile. The streets were an icy, dangerous mess. The next morning, all of the schools and most of the businesses were closed. It was the kind of day when everyone just sat at home, wrapped in blankets and drinking hot chocolate. Everyone but me. Since I'm a newspaper carrier, I go out in all sorts of weather. If the paper is published, which it *always* is, it must be delivered.

So on the first morning after the ice storm, I left at dawn. Good old Mom, she was right there with me. We often walk my route together; it gives us time to talk about what's going on in my life, school-wise. But that morning, Mom was strangely silent. We looked like a couple of mummies, dressed in warm hats and scarves and coats. It was almost too cold to talk, and we had to walk single file to navigate around the icy drifts. Pretty soon I zoned out, listening to the rhythm of our feet crunching in the icy snow.

Kindness makes a fellow feel good whether it's being done to him or by him.
Frank A. Clark

After a few blocks, I realized something was wrong. *I don't hear Mom's footsteps anymore!* I turned around. Mom had disappeared. One minute she was trailing about ten feet behind me—the next minute she was gone.

"Mom! Where are you?" I squinted though the gray dawn. Nothing. "Mom!"

I dropped the bag of papers and began to retrace my steps. "Mom!" My yells woke people up, and house lights started going on.

A few blocks away, I found Mom at the base of a snow bank. "Mom! Are you okay?"

Something was really wrong. Mom looked at me, but she couldn't talk. It looked like she'd slipped on a big ice patch. Seconds later, Dad came running up. "A neighbor just called me," he said. "They're calling an ambulance now."

At the hospital, we found out that Mom had broken her shoulder. "She'll need full-time care at home for at least twelve weeks," the doctor told us. "No cooking, no laundry, no cleaning. And no delivering papers."

As soon as Mom and Dad and I got home, we sat down for a family meeting with my two older sisters. "There's only one solution," I said. "Financially it's impossible for any of you to take a leave of absence from your jobs. I'll take a semester off from college and stay home with Mom."

The smallest good deed is better than the grandest good intention.

Duguet

"No," Mom objected. "You are going to continue your education—uninterrupted."

"But Mom, you can't even open a can of tuna. You heard what the doctor said. Until the break heals, the area is very fragile."

"I'll be fine." Mom was determined. "As soon as the swelling goes down I'll be as good as new."

Behind Mom's back, my sisters made motions indicating Mom's pain medication was affecting her judgment. Dad lifted his eyebrows in agreement.

Ding-dong!

Phew! Saved by the doorbell. I ran to answer it.

"Oh, hello, Mrs. Cobb." It was one of our neighbors.

Kindness begets kindness.
Greek Proverb

"Tell your mother that everything that needs to be done will be done," Mrs. Cobb said. "Each week, I'll bring a new volunteer sheet by so your mom will know who's doing what."

She handed me a piece of paper. On it were several columns, with headings like "Physical Therapy Visits," "Meals," "Ironing," "Laundry," and "Grocery Shopping." Names of people, some I didn't recognize, filled the spaces below.

"How did all these people find out about Mom's accident? It happened only a few hours ago."

Mrs. Cobb smiled. "When a friend is in need, news travels quickly. There are more volunteers than there are things to be done." She patted my cheek. "Your family's busy enough. Leave everything to those of us on the list."

After Mrs. Cobb left, I returned to Mom's side. I handed her the sheet and said just one word: "Withdrawals."

She understood, even if Dad and my sisters didn't.

Tenderness and kindness are not signs of weakness and despair, but manifestations of strength and resolution.

KAHLIL GIBRAN

That was a year ago. Now, Mom's charitable deeds don't bother me so much. I try to help her more than I used to, although my chocolate cakes never seem to be as moist as hers.

Maybe someday my "bank account" will be as full as Mom's. Until then I'm just living my life—one good deed at a time.

Return to Sender

BY JENNI MCMICHAEL

I stood with Daddy in the doorway as we watched the rain continue to fall. Drop after drop fell from the gray sky to join the floodwater rushing past the doorstep. A few minutes later, to everyone's relief, the rain slowly eased to a drizzle.

You have not lived a perfect day, even though you have earned your money, unless you have done something for someone who will never be able to repay you.
RUTH SMELTZER

That night I lay in bed, silently thanking God for protecting our home. Others hadn't been so blessed. Houses had been pushed off their foundations and into the river, smashed to bits. County shelters were overflowing with homeless people. Many had lost all their possessions. I couldn't just lie there and do nothing—I had to help. Throwing back the covers, I swung my feet over the side of the bed.

After rummaging though our cluttered craft room, I found a cardboard box. I would fill it in the morning. I crawled back into my bed and soon fell asleep.

The next day was Sunday. Before it was time to

leave for church, I dug through my closet. I pulled out some dolls I hadn't played with in years. Some little girl would be glad to have them. After going through a lot of my stuff, I found a pair of jeans that never quite fit, a shirt I really didn't like, and a Bible that had long ago been replaced by a newer one. I was proud of the way my box was filling up.

"Hey, David." I caught my little brother's arm as he dashed by. "I'm filling this box for Daddy to take to the shelter. It's for the people who lost everything in the flood yesterday. Do you want to put something in it?"

His gray-blue eyes were serious as I spoke, then he nodded.

He's a good little guy, I thought to myself as I watched him hurry to his room. I figured he'd grab one of his scratched-up trucks, but David surprised me when he returned with Muffin. Muffin was his favorite. The scraggly black-and-white stuffed dog wasn't new even when he came into David's possession. And since then he had somehow obtained a large mustard stain from a long-ago sandwich. All the same, he was David's favorite.

Guard well within yourself that treasure, kindness. Know how to give without hesitation, how to lose without regret, how to acquire without meanness.

George Sand

"*Muffin?*" I asked him. "Are you sure?" I remembered *my* gifts—those old dolls and too-long jeans. David was willing to sacrifice something he really loved.

"Thanks," I said, ashamed. I quickly tucked Muffin into the corner of the box.

Later that day, Daddy brought home an elderly couple who had barely escaped with their lives. They had spent the night in the shelter, not knowing if they still had a house. Exhausted, the man could hardly stand.

"Thank you, thank you," his wife kept murmering as we showed them to their room.

Over the next few weeks my parents helped them clean out their flooded house. Six feet of water had ruined almost everything, and a thick, sludgy mud now covered the yard and floor of the house.

The lady, Kim, took a liking to David immediately.

Remember there's no such thing as a small act of kindness. Every act creates a ripple with no logical end.

Scott Adams

"Your brother has made me smile again," Kim told me one day. "I only wish there was something I could give him . . . you know . . . so he'll remember us when all this is over."

"Oh, he won't need anything," I answered. "I can tell—he'll be your friend forever. David's like that."

"Yes, I suppose you're right. Even so . . ." Her voice trailed off.

I wasn't too surprised the next day when Kim showed up with a surprise for David.

"Hey, sugar!" she called to him, holding her hands behind her back. "Look! I got you something. I found it at the donation storehouse in the toy pile." David came close. I watched him smile as Kim offered him the toy.

A warm smile is the universal language of kindness.

William Arthur Ward

"I'm sorry it's not a new toy, David," she said.

But he didn't mind. He took from her hands the offered gift: a black-and-white stuffed dog—one with a mustard stain. Muffin.

"Thank you," David said.

That's incredible! I thought, watching David run off to his room to play. *Of all the toys, why Muffin? Why that ragged, stained dog?* But I had an idea.

I know now that whatever you give is what comes back to you. And the greater the sacrifice, the greater the return.

Freezing in the Sun

BY MICHELLE GARRARD

The couple was young and thin. The cardboard sign they carried was a torn scrap with black lettering: "Broke, homeless, please help. God bless." They stood at an intersection near one of Tucson's strip malls, by the left-turn lane where cars had to slow down. They had a young boy with them, a boy too old to be their child. My mom stopped.

A kind word is like a spring day.
RUSSIAN PROVERB

The wind in Tucson can bring the chill factor down. It was windy, and all three were wearing what looked like thin windbreakers. With their hair blowing, they all looked cold. My mom went into McDonald's and came out with $25 in gift certificates. She gave them to the couple, along with a quarter, and told them to call the Salvation Army for shelter that night. The little boy—he turned out to be the girl's brother—just looked down at the ground. He never said anything. He seemed to be frozen, both from the cold wind and from embarrassment.

When we got into our car and back on the road, I had a tight feeling in my stomach. Why were the three of them stranded? Had we done enough for them? As I listened to my mom's lecture on the dangers of giving too much cash to the homeless, I could not get out of my mind how cold they had looked. As I peppered my mom with questions, she finally replied in exasperation, "Well, Michelle, what do you want to do? We can't solve all the problems of the homeless. Where do you want to start?"

True kindness presupposes the faculty of imagining as one's own the suffering and joys of others.
André Gide

Somehow, at that moment, I knew where I wanted to start. "With coats," I said.

I explained my idea that night to my parents. I wanted to start a coat drive for the homeless of Tucson, Arizona. Mom and Dad said the best way to begin, since I was fifteen and it was already Thanksgiving, was to make it a drive for coats to be given to the Salvation Army. The Salvation Army in Tucson maintains a "Hospitality House" that has the system already in place to give coats to the homeless. I learned that they have a program called "Operation Deep Freeze" that goes into action when the temperature drops below thirty-five degrees on a clear night, or forty degrees on a rainy or windy night. I also learned from the manager of the Hospitality House that there is a daily population of between 1,000 and 2,500 homeless in Tucson. Approximately 235 to 250 will come to the Hospitality House on Deep Freeze days.

That weekend I started making posters. Both my church and my high school allowed me to print notices in their newsletters. I distributed my posters to local churches. I got my grandparents to help, and they distributed posters too. Then the calls began to come in. By Christmas, I had forty-four coats. One was a black leather, full-length, man's coat. We received raincoats and a lot of wool jackets. I hung each on a hanger, checked to make sure it was clean and had all of its buttons, and then took all forty-four down to Hospitality House with my dad.

One kind word can warm three winter months.
Japanese Proverb

The night we got there, over two hundred people had already checked themselves in. I don't know what I expected. Some looked like the family we had seen at the intersection, some were quite old, and some were teenage girls—girls who looked just like me.

The pile of forty-four coats had seemed like such a lot in my dad's trunk. But there were more than forty-four people at the Hospitality House. So when I won Miss Arizona Teenager the next year, I decided to make my coat drive into a year-long project. The terms of my reign required me to make "community service" appearances. Why not use those appearances to solicit coats?

Wearing the rhinestone tiara and the silk banner, I was able to waltz into local businesses and get permission to put up my posters. I enlisted my family's help again and wrote more notices for local churches and schools. This time, by spreading my net wider and starting earlier, I got 169 coats. It took two trips to the Salvation Army to deliver them all, and each trip required a caravan of two cars.

Last year I started even earlier and found new sources of help. I read a sign in a dry cleaner's window: "Arizona law allows clothes left for over ninety days to be disposed of at the option of the dry cleaner." That day I wrote the head of that business a letter. Later, he brought us three coats, four jackets, and ten heavy sweaters!

We make a living by what we get, but we make a life by what we give.
Norman MacEswan

My goal was 235 coats, the same number of people who went to Hospitality House that December night when I had only forty-four coats. When the coat drive was over, I counted 314 coats!

I don't know if even 314 coats were enough, but I do know that what Captain Dickinson of the Salvation Army told me kept me going: "Many of the homeless come to us with just the clothes they are wearing, and rarely does that include a coat."

The message on the torn cardboard sign I saw that raw November day included the words "God bless." God has blessed me: he sent me this work and my whole family has pitched in. My sister is taking over the drive this year while I'm away at college, so it will continue. My only regret is that I didn't get started earlier. Then that family I saw at the intersection could have had warm coats on that cold, windy night.

One of the most difficult things to give away is kindness, for it is usually returned.

Mark Ortman

The Goat Woman

BY CAROL GILLIS ZETTERBERG

The Goat Woman. My family attended church in the neighboring town where she lived; and sometimes as we drove by her shack huddled on the edge of a swampy field, we would see her outside, surrounded by the goats she tended. At other times we would see her on the street, dressed in a shabby brown coat and carrying two large shopping bags. I often wondered what was in those bags.

A bit of fragrance always clings to the hand that gives roses.
CHINESE PROVERB

Once when I was alone, walking down the street, I rounded a corner and almost collided with her. She was bent over a garbage can, and her long, dark, greasy hair, streaked with gray, hung in tangles around her face. On her feet were "shoes" of rubber inner-tube pieces tied together with string. She was muttering to herself, not making any sense.

There was a stench about her, but the smell was nothing compared to the clammy fear I felt when she turned her vacant eyes on mine and held me in her stare. I dashed past her, but from then on, whenever we drove past her shack, I felt a shiver run up my spine.

My father, though, never seemed to be put off by the Goat Woman, or by anyone else. Dad was superintendent of schools and was the bravest man I knew. Often I had seen him stop and talk and even teach a few wrestling holds to a group of tough guys who hung out on the street corner. I always hoped that some of Dad's courage would rub off on me.

Blessed is he who is kind to the needy.

Proverbs 14:21

Then something happened that made me face my fear and made me see the Goat Woman in a totally different way.

Easter morning I dressed in my new outfit and, with my brothers and sisters, piled into the car and headed for church.

I sat next to Dad in a pew close to the front, where I could watch my mom play the organ. The sound of the organ and the sweet fragrance of Easter lilies filled the air. I smoothed the flowered fabric of my new skirt and thought how beautiful everything was.

Gradually I became aware of a rustling and whispering throughout the church. I was wondering what it was when I felt someone squeezing in beside me. Turning, I could not believe my eyes. There, with her greasy hair, was the Goat Woman! What was the Goat Woman doing in my church?

Her smell blotted out the fragrance of the lilies. A wave of nausea swept over me at the thought of her filthy coat pressed so firmly against my beautiful new clothes. One of her shopping bags rested against my leg.

The rest of the service passed in a haze. I suppose the choir sang Handel's "Hallelujah Chorus," as they always did on Easter. I suppose the minister preached a sermon on the women going to Christ's empty tomb. I don't remember any of it. All I could think of was the Goat Woman at my side.

If I can stop one heart from breaking, I shall not live in vain; If I can ease one life the aching, Or cool one pain, Or help one fainting robin Unto his nest again, I shall not live in vain.

EMILY DICKINSON

When the service was over and the Goat Woman moved out into the aisle, I began to breathe more easily. But the Goat Woman's grasp on her bags must not have been firm enough. The shopping bags toppled over, and I finally found out what they held. Rotting apples, gnawed-over chicken bones, corncobs, orange peelings—slimy, disgusting garbage cascaded across the newly waxed floor of the church.

There was a collective gasp, then an awkward silence as people instinctively moved back. Wordlessly, the Goat Woman knelt down to pick up the mess. No one seemed to know what to do.

There is no better exercise for your heart than reaching down and helping to lift someone up.
Bernard Meltzer

Suddenly two figures were kneeling in the garbage. One was the Goat Woman, and the other was a well-dressed man. As he scooped up potato peelings, steak bones, and eggshells, he was talking quietly to her.

It was Dad. My dad. Kneeling in garbage while talking with a woman who smelled like goats, and acting like it was the most normal thing in the world. I blushed, half from embarrassment and half from pride that my dad had taken charge of things.

Suddenly the tension was broken. People relaxed and began talking, and some even helped out.

Soon everything was cleaned up, and the Goat Woman, her eyes downcast, turned to Dad and murmured, "Thank you. . . . it's for my goats."

"It must take a lot of time and work to find enough food for them," Dad said gently. Then he added, "Could we give you a ride home?"

The smile on her face could have lit up the stained glass windows.

With all seven of us in the car, we were pressed even closer than we had been in church. The funny thing was, I didn't notice the smell of the goats anymore. The woman I had thought repulsive complimented me on my new outfit. When we reached her house, Dad opened the car door for her. "Imagine," Mother said as we watched the Goat Woman amble across her cluttered yard, "she was quoting Shakespeare!"

As we pulled away, I watched the woman emptying the contents of her bags into the yard. Suddenly something my father had said to me a long time ago flashed into my mind, something that I didn't quite understand until that moment.

If someone were to pay you ten cents for every kind word you ever spoke and collect five cents for every unkind word, would you be rich or poor?
AUTHOR UNKNOWN

"Carol, every human being has a divine spark," he had said. "God breathed something of himself into each of us. If you look hard enough, you'll find it."

Later we learned that the Goat Woman had been a teacher. Years ago when her fiancé left her, something inside her had crumbled, and she had retreated into a strange world of her own.

This story had a happy ending. Through the county mental health clinic, Dad helped arrange for a medical evaluation of the Goat Woman. A chemical imbalance was discovered. With proper medication, she was able to live an independent and productive life.

That Goat Woman, instead of being a witch, turned out to be an angel who helped teach me that we are all made in God's image. Sometimes we just have to look hard to see it.

Kindness is in our power, even when fondness is not.

Samuel Johnson

The Kindness of True Friends

Prom Tag-Along

by April Stier

Sometimes good things come out of bad. You always hear people saying that, but it's what happened to me. If it hadn't been for my disastrous senior prom, I might never have connected with my best friend, Heather.

Heather and I were friends in high school, but we weren't "best" friends. At the beginning of my senior year, I had a different best friend, Sara. In my kitchen late one night, she dropped a bomb on me.

> *He who sows courtesy reaps friendship, and he who plants kindness gathers love.*
>
> Saint Basil

"Nathan asked me to the prom!"

My stomach dropped. Was Sara serious? Nathan was not only gorgeous, he was the most intelligent and talented guy in our high school. I had a serious crush on him our entire senior year. Everyone thought he would ask *me* to prom. How could he have asked my best friend?

"What did you tell him?" I asked.

"I said yes." Sara looked at me. "You're not mad, are you? You said you didn't like him anymore, so I didn't think you'd mind. You don't, do you?"

My mind whirled. I *had* told her a week ago that I no longer liked Nathan, accepting the fact that we would never be anything more than friends. But could I really watch him escort my best friend to prom?

"Of course I don't mind," I said, forcing a smile.

The reality of the situation didn't sink in until I slipped into bed that night. Sara had said "yes" to the question that I constantly fantasized Nathan would ask me. *How could she? So what if I told her last week I was over him. Doesn't she realize it takes more than a week to get over feelings that strong?*

My heart felt like a brick in my chest. Sara and I had made a pact that dates or not, we were going to the prom together. No one was left for me to ask, and I had no hope of anyone else asking me. I closed my eyes. My greatest fear had come true: I was going to my senior prom alone.

Let no one ever come to you without leaving better and happier. Be the living expression of God's kindness: kindness in your face, kindness in your eyes, kindness in your smile.

Mother Teresa

Oh, God . . . why is this happening to me? Tears soaked my pillow until I fell into a restless sleep.

The next few days were awful. I avoided Sara; and when I saw Nathan in my classes and at lunch, I pretended that everything was fine.

One day, Sara caught me after school.

"April, I know you've been avoiding me. I don't want a guy to come between us. How can we fix this?"

I looked at the floor. "I don't know."

"What are your plans for prom?" she asked.

"I'm not sure if I'm going anymore, since you and I were supposed to go together," I said, giving her a pointed look.

Sara chewed her lip. Then her face lit up like she had an idea. "I know! We can still go together!"

"Huh?"

As in filling a vessel drop by drop, there is at last a drop which makes it run over; so in a series of kindnesses there is at last one which makes the heart run over.

SAMUEL JOHNSON

"After Nathan picks me up, we can come get you and go to the restaurant. Then we can hang out together. Come on . . . there will be lots of people at the prom stag anyway—you'll still have fun!"

"Um . . . I guess. . . ."

"Perfect!" Sara said, giving me a hug. "Maybe we'll go with Heather and Ashley and their dates. It'll be a blast!"

As she walked away, I couldn't help wondering what I had just gotten myself into.

Prom day finally arrived, and I rushed from my hair appointment back home to get ready. After taking extra care with my makeup, I slipped into my long, navy blue dress and pulled on my shoes. I saw Nathan's car pull into my driveway through the window. With one last look in the mirror, I tucked a few curls into place, took a deep breath, and walked into the living room.

My heart fluttered when I saw Nathan in his black tuxedo. Sara looked beautiful in her pale green dress. It felt a little strange at first; but we made some small talk until our friend, Heather, and her date, Seth, showed up. Heather introduced everyone to Seth, and after a barrage of pictures, we headed to the cars.

What wisdom can you find that is greater than kindness?

Jean Jacques Rousseau

"One more stop before we go to the restaurant," said Nathan, as I climbed into the back seat. "We need to go to Aric's house for more pictures." Aric was our friend Ashley's date. I sighed. *Great. Pictures of me and three happy couples.*

As we arrived at Aric's house, my jaw dropped. A limousine was parked by the garage. I'd always dreamed of going to prom in a limo.

"It only seats four," I heard Nathan say to Sara.

I did the math. Including Aric and Ashley, I made five. Nathan couldn't have missed that, right? I mean, he *knew* I was coming. *Surely they'll make room for me—Sara won't leave me alone.* An uneasy feeling gnawed at my stomach as I smiled through the pictures. When it was time to leave, Sara came over.

"The limo only seats four," she said, with no emotion.

Tears pricked my eyes. I felt like I had a huge "L" on my forehead—one that *didn't* stand for limo.

Heather spoke up. "April, you can ride with us."

Without a word, I followed Heather to Seth's small sports car. I gathered my dress and scrunched into the back seat. As we drove to the restaurant, silent tears streamed down my face. This was supposed to be a night I'd always remember, but it had turned into a cruel joke.

Kindness is love, but perhaps greater than love . . . Kindness is good will. Kindness says, "I want you to be happy."
Randolph Ray

Dinner was really awkward. Sara and Nathan barely spoke to me, and no one said a word about the limo. I felt like a complete reject. The only person who even seemed to know I was there was Seth, who kept making faces at me from the other end of the table. Thankfully, that lightened things up a little. Seth even paid for my dinner.

At the prom, I felt numb. Nathan ignored me; he seemed too captivated by Sara. I danced and tried to have a good time, but it was hard. I felt so hurt and alone. When yet another slow dance began to play, I walked back to our table. Slumping in my chair, I watched the couples on the dance floor. *God, this is the worst night of my life! Nothing good can possibly come from this.*

Then something incredible happened. Seth walked up to me and held out his hand. "Would you like to dance?"

The words of kindness are more healing to a drooping heart than balm or honey.
SARAH FIELDING

Too shocked to answer, I simply nodded my head. He led me onto the dance floor.

"How are you doing?" he whispered.

"What do you mean?"

"I can see you're having a tough night," he said. "But you've really handled it with class."

I didn't know what to say. "Thanks, Seth."

Seth's words meant a lot to me. For the first time that night I felt myself relax. *Maybe something good will come from tonight after all,* I thought.

The song ended, and a fast song blared through the speakers. Heather joined us out on the floor.

"Thanks for dancing with Seth, April. It gave

me a chance to run around and take some photos for the yearbook." She motioned to her camera sitting on the table.

"C'mon," Seth said. "We're wasting some great tunes! Let's dance!"

So we did. The three of us. We hung out together for the rest of the night, and we had a great time. I talked and laughed so much with Heather that night; it was one of those rare instances where you just "click" with someone and you can't help but be happy. Best of all, by the time prom was over I realized the Nathan and Sara situation didn't matter so much anymore. God had given me a new friendship with Seth and a better-than-ever friendship with Heather.

Rare as is true love, true friendship is still rarer.

Francois, Duc de la Rochefoucauld

In some ways, my senior prom was a true disaster. But looking back, I wouldn't trade it for anything. Good things *can* come from bad, and I have my best friend Heather to prove it.

Lucky Break

by Brinck Slattery

Saint Andrew's. Ever since I was a little kid, I'd wanted to come to this coed boarding school. Now that I was finally here, I was a little nervous. It was the first time I'd be living on my own, far from home. I was counting on football to help me fit in and make friends.

One kind act will teach more love of God than a thousand sermons.
Author Unknown

I tried to act confident as I descended the stairs to the locker room to get suited up for the first day of pre-season football camp. A lot of the other guys obviously knew each other and were laughing and talking, catching up on what had happened over the summer. I picked up my pads and helmet, then found a bench and began lacing up my cleats.

"Hi! I'm Nick. I'm a senior. I'm a lineman too. You'll be working with me."

I looked up to see a guy with huge shoulders and thick arms. A *senior?* Back home, seniors didn't talk to freshmen.

"See you on the field!" Nick said. He vanished up the stairs before I could say anything.

At practice, I did all the things linemen do. I squatted. I did forward rolls. I stayed in my stance for a ridiculous amount of time. I ran endless sprints and rehearsed plays over and over.

On the last afternoon of camp, Nick, who turned out to be one of the team's co-captains, clapped me on the shoulder. "Hey, Brinck. I've got good news. I talked to Coach and we want you to be our starting offensive tackle. Congratulations!"

Me? Starting? This was a big deal for a freshman. Big pressure too. For a split second, I wished I were back home where I could talk to my old friends about the news.

Kind words can be short and easy to speak, but their echoes are truly endless.
Mother Teresa

Our first game was a pre-season scrimmage. We climbed onto the school bus for the two-hour ride to Woodbridge, a school downstate. I sat alone, but I didn't mind. As the flat Delaware landscape sped past my window, I went over plays in my head. When we arrived, I was ready.

Woodbridge kicked off, and we got the ball on our thirty-yard line. Our offense ran three plays, and I blocked defensive players right and left. After our third down, as I moved back toward the huddle, I felt a hand slap my back and shove me. It was

Woodbridge's defensive tackle, just being nasty. Suddenly I was falling forward. I flung out my hands to brace myself. *Ouch!*

No big deal. I'll get him back on the next play.

Ten seconds later I realized that I couldn't move my fingers and my wrist was swelling. I raised my good hand and Coach Hyde subbed me out.

"That arm doesn't look good, Brinck."

Somebody drove me to the emergency room, where the doctor told me I had broken my right arm badly. The X ray showed I had fractured both bones at the wrist. I also had nerve damage, which explained the numb sensation in my fingers.

On the ride back to school, I was miserable. I had a temporary cast from just above my knuckles to my armpit, and it itched like crazy. The pain was so bad I could hardly think straight.

I had injured myself before the school year had even begun, and it wasn't even during a play! I felt so humiliated. I had let Coach and the team down. My football season was ruined.

The small change of human happiness lies in the unexpected friendly word.
Author Unknown

Because of my broken arm, I decided not to go to the get-acquainted square dance the night before classes started. No way did I want to explain my injury to a whole crowd of people I didn't know. To make things worse, I had broken my writing arm. My left-handed writing was a mess, and all I could do typing with my left hand was hunt-and-peck. On the second day of class, my English teacher tossed my first graded journal on my desk. It looked like it was bleeding red ink. An *F*! English was supposed to be one of my strengths. *What else can go wrong?*

Friendship is one of the sweetest joys of life. Many might have failed beneath the bitterness of their trial had they not found a friend.
Charles Spurgeon

On Wednesday, I went to an orthopaedic surgeon to get my permanent cast. By that weekend, I was exhausted, confused, and really down. Maybe Saint Andrew's wasn't the right place for me. As laughter broke out across the hall, I became even more worried. *What if they're laughing at me? What am I doing here?* While I'd been nursing my arm, everyone else had spent their first weekend at school staying up late, having fun, and getting to know each other.

As I lay on my bed, feeling homesick and missing my old friends, I heard a knock on the door.

"Brinck?"

It was Nick.

"Hey, I just wanted to tell you that I'm sorry about everything that's happened. Don't worry. All this is going to work out fine."

Easy for him to say. "Thanks," I mumbled.

"No, seriously! We prayed for you this morning at chapel. Good things can come out of bad situations. I've seen it happen more than once."

I sat up as he turned to go. "Hey, thanks," I said. "Listen, when does your cast come off?"

"End of October, I hope."

"Well, when it comes off, do you want to join the Polar Bear Club?"

"The Polar Bear Club?"

"Once a month we jump in the pond at 6:50 in the morning."

"Are you *crazy*?"

Nick explained that the Polar Bear Club goes out and jumps in Noxontown Pond every month, regardless of ice and snow. Once a year, in February, the club raises pledges for the Special Olympics and then travels to Rehobeth Beach to jump in the Atlantic Ocean. "It's an awesome feeling—you *have* to try it!"

The greatest thing a man can do for his heavenly Father is to be kind to some of his other children.
HENRY DRUMMOND

I laughed. "Okay, you're talking me into it." Nick seemed really happy. *Maybe I can make a friend or two here, in spite of this arm*, I thought as Nick headed back to his room.

When I left my dorm the next morning, I tried to stay upbeat. As the day unfolded, I realized my cast wasn't keeping me from making friends; in fact, it started to *attract* them. When I dropped my books in a sad attempt to carry them myself, students offered to help me. Soon I was walking to class with new friends. Guys in the dorm saw me trying, slowly, to separate my lights from my darks, and offered to help me do my laundry. My English teacher finally picked up on my complete inability to write left-handedly and offered to tutor me outside of class.

Things were going pretty well until U. S. History. I was running late; and as I squeezed into my chair, I sent a stack of books that belonged to the girl next to me clattering to the floor. I could feel my face turning red.

If the world is cold, make it your business to build fires.
Horace Traubel

"I'm so sorry," I said, bending down to pick up the books.

"No problem," she said. "Cool cast. Can I sign it?"

Before long, *everyone* wanted to sign my cast. By the end of the week my broken arm was covered with scribbled autographs, funny drawings, and words of encouragement.

Finally, at the end of October, my cast came off. After I got back to school from the doctor's, I ran into Nick.

"Big Polar Bear jump tomorrow morning! Are you going to be there?"

"Oh yeah!"

The cold dew bit at my bare feet as I stomped down to the dock. My thin T-shirt was *not* keeping me warm. *This is insane*, I thought. Then, without a word, people began jumping into the pond.

It's now or never!

I got a running start and flew off the dock. The water was *freezing*. Steam rose off of us as we got out of the pond on that misty October morning. People laughed and shouted, waking up anyone foolish enough to try to sleep through the jump. I was so happy.

There is nothing better than the encouragement of a good friend.
Katherine Hathaway

It's amazing to think about how many friends I made my freshman year because of that stupid cast. Good things *can* come out of bad. It happens all the time.

The Guitar

BY ERIC PANZA

A Taylor. Model 314. It was right there in the catalog. My dream guitar.

"It's a beauty," Ron said, eyeing my selection. Meanwhile, he was drooling over a Taylor on another page.

Ron and I were always talking about guitars. He and his wife, Patty, were the leaders of our church youth group, and I was one of the regulars. I usually came about half an hour early to the Bible study they held at their house so Ron and I could jam on our guitars before everyone else got there. That night, though, we were planning our custom-made Taylors.

Kindness in words creates confidence. Kindness in thinking creates profoundness. Kindness in giving creates love.
LAO-TSE

"Patty and I decided we're going to start saving for one," Ron told me. "Why don't you save up too?"

My heart raced. *Could I actually do it?* Taylors were so expensive, the Porsches of guitars. The bottom of the line started at around two thousand dollars. I did a quick mental calculation of my income and my expenses. Money had been tight since I graduated from high school and moved out on my own. But I probably could cut back on extras. *Okay*, I thought. *With a little planning and saving, I might be able to swing a base model in about six months*.

"You know what?" I told Ron. "I'm going to do it!"

I was psyched. I started saving right away, and after a few weeks I had around two hundred dollars. Not as much as I'd hoped, but I was making progress. I even promised my old guitar to some friends, Aaron and Vonda, who planned to use it for the youth group they led at another church. They'd only been married two years, and now they were expecting a baby. They didn't have a dime to spend on a guitar.

In this world it is not what we take up but what we give up that makes us rich.

Henry Ward Beecher

"Oh, Eric, that's so great!" Vonda said when I told her the news. "The kids in our group will be *so* excited!"

"Happy I can help," I told her. "I'll give you a call before long and bring it over."

All around, this was going to be a good deal for everyone.

A couple of months later, Ron got his Taylor. It was awesome! Now, I wanted mine more than ever. *Keep saving*, I told myself. *If Ron and Patty can do it, so can you.*

I knew Ron and Patty were almost as short on cash as I was. They'd been hit with expensive repairs on their house, and then Ron's dad died of cancer. They racked up some stiff bills from all the trips they took to Florida to help out. But they'd saved every penny, and Patty even worked extra shifts.

After that, I cut back as much as I could, trying to save money. It meant a lot less fast food, a lot more macaroni and cheese. And I had to really think before I bought a CD or went to a movie. But it wasn't so bad. Like always, when I was lonely or worried, I'd pick up my guitar and start playing. Music always helped me relax and put things in perspective.

Greatness lies in the faithful performance of the small acts of kindness that God has made possible for us.
Sidney Greenberg

But as the months went by, my finances took a hit. I worked a couple of jobs, but as if everyday expenses weren't enough, there was insurance and an old car loan to pay. Then my van broke down. Thanks to all the unexpected bills, my savings account statement once again read "$0." I guess I didn't realize how much living on my own would cost.

I finally had to admit it. *It's going to be a long time before I can afford a Taylor. Maybe even years*. I'd have to put my dream on long-term hold.

Then I thought of Aaron and Vonda. They were so excited about getting my old guitar. And I'd given them my word. Every time I saw them, they talked about how much the kids in their youth group would love the guitar and how they were looking forward to using it at services and retreats. I didn't have the heart to disappoint them. I finally made arrangements to bring it over to their house.

I had mixed emotions as I placed my guitar in its case for the last time. I'd made some good music over the years with it. *It'll work out*, I tried to convince myself. *Most every place I go there's a guitar I can borrow*.

The true meaning of life is to plant trees, under whose shade you do not expect to sit.
Nelson Henderson

As I pulled into Aaron and Vonda's driveway, I looked at my guitar, sitting on the seat next to me. The case was battered from all those nights at camp, our family vacations, even my trip to Mexico. *Lord, I can't remember the last time I've been without it*. For a split second, I considered turning back. *Aaron and Vonda don't know I'm here yet. . . . I can turn around and go home*.

I shook off the temptation to back out. As I grabbed the case and headed for the front door, I couldn't help thinking of Mom. She'd supported us by working as a hospice nurse, taking care of patients who were dying. I knew the job was hard on her emotionally. I saw her many times praying for those families, their pain becoming hers. Yet, when I asked why she kept doing it, she just said, "Believe me, Eric. Everything I've given has been returned to me tenfold."

I sighed. My nights were sure going to be lonely without this guitar. *Okay, God, I just can't get over the feeling that this is what you want me to do. Here goes.*

Aaron and Vonda were really excited, and I thought I brushed off the questions about my "other guitar" pretty well. I didn't want them to feel bad or refuse my gift. "Eric, this is so nice of you!" Vonda said, hugging me as I left that night. "I can hardly wait to try it out."

It is futile to judge a kind deed by its motives. Kindness can become its own motive. We are made kind by being kind.
Eric Hoffer

It was a long drive back to my place. It's funny, though. Logic told me I should feel a loss. After all, it was like I'd just said good-bye to my best friend. But I felt great. I kept replaying the look on Aaron and Vonda's faces and how they fingered my guitar like *it* was a Taylor. I knew I'd made the right decision.

Still, I found myself going earlier than ever to Ron and Patty's for youth group. Ron always let me jam on his Taylor, and it felt so good. I loved the soft harmonies rushing through my fingers. I loved the way the music helped me center my thoughts on God.

"Hey, Eric," Ron asked one evening. "How come you don't bring your guitar over anymore?" He knew I hadn't been able to afford the Taylor, but he hadn't seen my old guitar, either.

"Uh, someone else has it now," I said, hoping it would sound like I just loaned it out. I didn't want to lie, but I also didn't want to make a big deal over giving my guitar away.

Friendship—
pure, unselfish
friendship,
All through life's
allotted span,
Nurtures,
strengthens,
widens, lengthens,
Man's relation-
ship with man.
Author Unknown

But Ron wouldn't drop it. I finally had to come clean. "Actually, I gave it way," I told him. "I promised it to some friends and I didn't want to disappoint them. Do you think I could borrow your old one?"

Ron looked stunned. "Of course, Eric! You can take it home tonight. I'm sorry it isn't much."

Back home, I got Ron's old guitar out and started playing. *Twang!* This guitar was definitely not a Taylor, but I was thankful to have something to play again.

One night a couple months later, I came to youth group at Ron's house at my usual early time.

"Hi, Eric! Let's practice. Come on into the living room."

I have wept in the night for the shortness of sight that to somebody's need made me blind; But I never have yet felt a tinge of regret for being a little too kind.
Author Unknown

I sat down on a chair, and Ron motioned to his Taylor, sitting in its case beside the coffee table. "Go ahead and get it out for me," he said.

Ron and Patty sat across from me on the couch. They were looking at me funny. *What's gotten into them?* I wondered as I opened the case.

"Hey, what happened to your guitar?" I asked.

I knew Ron's guitar like the back of my hand. This was different. It was a Taylor Model 414. It had rich, rose-colored spruce on top and beautiful wood on the sides. I looked up at Ron and Patty, who were smiling so big I thought they were going to pass out.

"It's not *my* Taylor," Ron said. "It's *yours*."

I froze. *Am I dreaming?* I ran my hand over the highly polished neck, fingering the mother-ofpearl inlays. *It's even better than the Taylor I originally picked out!*

"We know you loved your guitar," Patty said. "When we found out the nice thing you did with it, we wanted you to have your own Taylor. So we had one specially made."

"Go ahead," said Ron. "Play!"

I looked up in disbelief. This was an incredibly expensive gift. *I can't possibly accept this. I have to give it back.*

I opened my mouth to refuse the gift, but I saw a familiar look on Ron and Patty's faces. I could tell they were feeling the same way I did on the way home from Aaron and Vonda's: that feeling of sacrificing something, just because you know it's the right thing to do. I looked down at the guitar, remembering Mom's words: *Give and it will come back to you tenfold.*

You are best to yourself when you are good to others.
Author Unknown

Tenfold? I thought. *Make that ten*-million *fold!*

"Thanks," I said. "This is the best gift ever." And I wasn't just talking about the guitar.

Blind Date

BY FELICIA SILCOX

My younger sister, Eileen, got all the looks in our family. I mean, guys drool when they see her coming. So when it came time for our high school's fall formal, Eileen easily landed a date—with the cutest guy in her freshman class.

But Dad, an Army sergeant who bounces a quarter off our bed sheets to make sure we've pulled them tightly enough, had laid down the rule. Eileen couldn't go to her first big dance unless I, her older sister, also went. *Great.*

Friendship improves happiness and abates misery, by the doubling of our joy and the dividing of our grief.
MARCUS TULLIUS CICERO

For me, finding a date was a major challenge. I'd always figured that playing ball with the guys in the neighborhood was more fun than chasing some heartthrob, who'd melt as soon as he saw my sister. Sure, boys were nice, but I could survive without one just fine, thank you.

"Can't you do *something* to get a date?" My sister's soft brown eyes brimmed with tears. I couldn't stand to see Eileen hurting.

So I unclenched my sweaty palms, cleaned the

smudges off my glasses, and asked Butch, a stock boy in the store where I work after school. He flirted with everybody—I figured he was my best shot. But Charm-Boy mumbled something about having a serious girlfriend. *Right*.

Next I asked Tommy, the laid-back skateboarder who lives across the street. He tousled my hair and grinned. "I can't take you to a dance, goofball. You're like my sister!"

How many people stop because so few say "Go!"
Charles Swindoll

I even called one of my cousins (yuck!), but he was taking someone else.

Then I called Mary Ann. Everyone in the world should be lucky enough to have a friend like Mary Ann. "No problem," she said. "I'll tell my date, Mike, to ask one of his friends to go with you. We'll double! It'll be fun."

A date with a guy I've never met? What if we hate each other? I wouldn't call that fun. But I could stand anything for one night, if it would make Eileen happy.

Several days passed before I heard that Mike, who goes to a different school, found my blind date. I didn't know how he did it, who the mystery man was, or what he was like. I figured I'd find out soon enough.

There was, however, one small problem. Mike's

buddy worked bagging groceries until 7:00 P.M. on Saturday nights. No big deal, we'd just be a little late, that's all. I ran everything by Dad, and a thousand questions later, my sister got the green light.

How far you go in life depends on your being tender with the young, compassionate with the aged, sympathetic with the striving and tolerant of the weak and strong. Because someday in life you will have been all of these.
George Washington Carver

The night of the dance, Eileen's date arrived early and pinned on her corsage. Mom ran for her camera, and Eileen flashed me a radiant smile as her crush held open the front door for her. I was so happy for her.

I touched up my makeup and hair, then sat down to do my history homework while I waited for my date to show up. I waited and waited. I outlined a chapter. I watched the clock.

"Young lady," my dad said, after nearly two hours. "I'm depending on you to keep an eye on your sister at that dance. Your friends should have picked you up by now!"

Almost 9:30. The dance had started at 8:00. *How could I be in such a mess just by doing a favor for my sister?* I twisted my bangs. I called Mary Ann and got no answer. *Where can they be?*

Finally, my mother announced that she saw headlights in our driveway. I ran to the front door. There stood Mary Ann, looking paler than I'd ever seen her. "Your date didn't show," she whispered, her eyes wide. "We couldn't find him anywhere."

"I'm dead."

Mary Ann pulled me outside. "Listen. Mike and I talked about this on the way over. We promised you a date, so he'll be your date tonight and I'll just tag along."

A real friend is one who walks in when the rest of the world walks out.
Walter Winchell

"Are you *crazy*? I can't steal your date!"

"I won't have it any other way. Now hurry up, we're wasting time!"

Before I knew it, Mike was striding into our living room and heartily shaking hands with my father, who had risen from his recliner.

Somehow I choked out, "Dad, this is Mike."

"Glad to meet you, son." Dad scanned Mike's short haircut, clean-shaven face, and crisp white shirt. I could tell he was impressed, especially when Mike looked him in the eye and apologized for being late.

"We'd better hurry," Mary Ann sang out, hustling us toward the front door.

All of us jammed into the front seat of Mike's old Chevy. Bad thinking on my part, especially when I saw my mother peeking out of the kitchen window. *If she counts only three heads in the car . . .*

"Turn on your headlights! Quick!" I said.

Mike caught on and burned rubber backing the car into the street. We had cleared the first hurdle, but another waited.

The value of compassion cannot be over-emphasized. Anyone can criticize. It takes a true believer to be compassionate. No greater burden can be borne by an individual than to know no one cares or understands.
ARTHUR H. STAINBACK

Our school was very strict, and because the dance was formal, all our teachers formed a receiving line at the entrance to the gym. We had to "properly introduce" our escorts before we could get into the dance. No escort, no entrance.

This time I took a stand. "Okay, you two. I really appreciate what you did for me back there. But we're here now. There's no way you're not going in as a couple. I'll just hang out here until the teachers leave and maybe slip in later."

"Tell you what," Mike said, positioning himself between us and extending his elbows. "I'll escort *both* of you to the dance."

Fixing a beauty queen smile on her face, Mary Ann went first, her left arm linked with Mike's right. I hooked him with my right arm and swept along behind.

Amazingly, none of the teachers stopped to ask

us questions. We weren't the only ones who'd arrived late, and the noisy mob of students in line provided good cover. We moved fast.

At the end of the line towered my biology teacher, who had once threatened to chloroform me if I didn't stop talking in her class. She looked like she could play linebacker for the Rams.

At the part of the introduction where I announced, "I'd like you to meet my date, Mike," her eyes darkened. Her head snapped toward Mary Ann, who was melting into the crowd.

If you were arrested for kindness, would there be enough evidence to convict you?
Author Unknown

"Then who . . . ?" she sputtered. Mike yanked me past her. I didn't look back.

The senior class had transformed the gym into a Japanese tea garden, complete with hanging lanterns, bamboo plants, painted silk screen, and a wooden bridge that arched across a pond of blue cellophane. We found a table at the far edge of the dance floor, and I took a seat. I watched all the couples, dancing and eating and talking together. *What am I doing here?* I thought.

"Care to dance?" It was Mike, asking me. *Me.*

"Oh, no, I . . ."

"Come on, you're my date!"

One who knows how to show and to accept kindness will be a friend better than any possession.
Sophocles

Mike led me onto the dance foor. Across the crowd, I caught my sister's eye, and she waved. She was laughing and clapping, having a blast. She looked so beautiful. The music slowed, and she began dancing with her date, eyes closed, still smiling ear to ear. I sighed. *Maybe there is something to this whole heartthrob thing.*

Mike danced one dance with me, then one with Mary Ann. He kept that up all night, right up to the last song. True friend that she was, Mary Ann had saved my evening from becoming a total disaster. And Mike, who took us both out for burgers after the dance, handled the whole event with the grace and polish of a real knight in shining armor. It turned out to be a wonderful dance, not just for my beautiful and charming sister, but for me too.

That night, when Mike and Mary Ann pulled into the driveway to drop me off, Mike made a crazy proposal. "Hey, Felicia! Want to come to *prom* with Mary Ann and me?"

"Yeah! How about it?" Mary Ann said.

I laughed. "Sure," I said. "I'll go to prom with you guys. But I think I'll find my own date."

The Power of Love

BY YOLANDA MARIE ADAMS

By the time I was thirteen, I'd known so much difficulty in my life that the taunts of the other kids at school shouldn't have stung. But their cruelty cut me deeply, leaving a hurt that wouldn't go away.

A word of kindness is seldom spoken in vain. It can be and is often treasured by the recipient for life.
GEORGE D. PRENTICE

"Jingle bells, Yolanda smells!" One autumn afternoon the insults got to be too much, maybe because I knew there was some truth to them. I ran from the school grounds, my ratty old sneakers slap-slapping on the pavement. "That's right," one boy yelled, "go home to the crazy lady!"

I turned onto my street, my footsteps slowing. Where was I running to? It wasn't as if our house were any sort of refuge. I stopped in front of the two prettiest houses on the block. They looked as neat and well cared for as the two girls I'd seen step out their front doors to walk side by side to school together. *It's not as if I have a place like one of those to go home to*, I thought. *Not anymore*.

Once I, too, had lived in a cozy home with

parents who loved me, a few years earlier, in Los Angeles. Dad had worked hard to provide for us and so had Mom, but she always made time to sit me on her lap and sing to me. Nothing, in those days, had seemed more beautiful to me than my mother's voice.

Then my great-grandmother and great-aunt fell ill. Looking after them and my brothers and sisters and me, Mom got overloaded. I guess she broke. One day she was taken away to the state hospital. Years later I found out she'd been subjected to massive drug therapy, but all I knew then was that when she came back, she wasn't Mom. Gone were the sweet songs, swallowed up by babbling that could escalate, without warning, into shouting.

Make sure that nobody pays back wrong for wrong, but always try to be kind to each other and to everyone else.
1 Thessalonians 5:15

Dad had moved our family here to La Puente, California, when I was ten, thinking the small-town atmosphere would be easier on Mom. But she hadn't gotten any better. She'd stay parked on the couch for hours, staring blankly at the TV, ignoring the dirty laundry and dishes. Those were her good days. On her bad days, she'd go outside without clothes on, yelling at anyone who tried to come near. Even with the long hours he put in at the sheriff's department,

Dad couldn't afford a full-time babysitter for us kids. So whenever Mom went into the hospital, we were sent to stay with various relatives in south-central L.A.

Kindness is more important than wisdom, and the recognition of this is the beginning of wisdom.
THEODORE RUBIN

Between all those different homes, I never really fit in anywhere. At school I was a loner, a convenient target for the other kids to pick on. I learned that adults couldn't protect me. I had to hide within myself, to withdraw into a kind of box where nothing could touch me.

Wanting to slip into that hiding place again, out of reach of those school ground taunts, I turned away from the pretty houses and resignedly started for my own. "Hey, wait up!" I heard someone call from down the street. Two sets of footsteps quickened behind me. *Probably guys wanting to tease me*. I picked up my pace. "Please, Yolanda?" I glanced over my shoulder.

Behind me were the two girls who lived in those houses I'd been admiring. They looked so perfect with their stylish clothes and shining hair, it made me feel more ashamed than ever about my uncombed hair and unwashed clothes. I ran inside, past my mom on the couch, to my bedroom.

The next morning on my walk to school, the same two girls fell in step beside me. "I'm Terrie Silva," said the dark-haired one, her eyes as sparkly as her glasses. "And that's Debbie Powell."

"Hi," the blond girl said softly. I was so stunned that they weren't backing away from me that I couldn't say a word.

I expect to pass through this world but once; any good thing therefore that I can do, or any kindness that I can show to any fellow creature, let me do it now; let me not defer or neglect it, for I shall not pass this way again.
Stephan Grellet

"We've seen you around," Terrie said. Then, her gaze locking on mine, she announced, "We're going to be your friends."

Not once in the years I'd been shuttling between L. A. and La Puente had someone said anything like that to me.

Wherever I went from then on, Debbie and Terrie were with me. Walking to school, in the hallways, in the cafeteria, I was never alone anymore. The boys in my class still jeered, even at Terrie and Debbie. "Why are you hanging out with Stinky?" I'd hang my head, wishing I could disappear. But Debbie would tuck her arm in mine, and Terrie would declare boldly, "Her name is Yolanda. And she's our friend."

There was that word again: *friend*. It had been so

long since I'd had one, I had forgotten what it was like. I sensed that what Terrie and Debbie were offering me was good, but I didn't really understand how to accept it. Still, it was hard to resist their determined efforts. When Terrie had Debbie and me over to make oatmeal cookies, and Mrs. Silva welcomed me with a hug, for a moment it was like I was part of a real family again. The next week we went to Debbie's to watch a movie. And Debbie's mom was just as sweet as she was.

When I started going to church with Terrie and Debbie and their parents, I noticed the sidelong glances and whispers from some of the other parishioners. Was it because I was the only black person there? Or because my clothes were shabby? I cringed in the pew, the walls of my box beginning to close in on me again. Then the pastor, Reverend Kutz, came and shook my hand. "Don't mind those people," he told me. "They don't know who you are. But God in his love does, and together we will teach the others." Though I wasn't quite sure what he meant, the kindness in his voice reached through my hurt and shame. I sat up a little straighter.

One can pay back the loan of gold, but one lies forever in debt to those who are kind.

Malayan Proverb

One rainy afternoon about a year after they had sought me out, Debbie and Terrie were walking me home. We were almost at my house when my mom ran out at us in a rage. "Mom, don't," I pleaded. She ignored me. "Go away!" Mom screamed at Debbie and Terrie. "And don't come back. No one wants you here!"

Terrified, they took off. Mom pushed me inside and slammed the door. I felt shut in so tight I could hardly breathe.

If someone is too tired to give you a smile, leave one of your own, because no one needs a smile as much as those who have none to give.
RAPHAEL HIRSCH

Later, my mother dozed off in front of the TV, and I was finally able to slip out. But I only got as far as the edge of the street. *Where can I go?* I thought, sinking down on the curb. *Debbie and Terrie won't want anything to do with me now. Mom chased away the only thing in my life that was good.*

The next morning Debbie and Terrie were waiting to walk to school with me. "I didn't think you'd be back," I said. "Not after my mom . . ."

"We're your friends," Debbie said. Terrie added, "No matter what." I took their outstretched hands, but I knew I didn't deserve their friendship.

Then one Sunday the sermon really spoke to me. "Jesus loves you. You don't have to be perfect. He won't give up on you, no matter what."

Like Terrie and Debbie? I thought, glancing at

them on either side of me.

"He loves you so much that he will bear your hurt and sorrow for you. You just have to open your heart to him."

I stared up at the figure in the stained glass window above the altar. Then I bowed my head. "Please, Jesus, I need you," I whispered.

We must be as courteous to a man as we are to a picture, which we are willing to give the advantage of a good light.

Ralph Waldo Emerson

All at once, from that figure above came an outpouring so intense that momentarily everything else, including the troubles in my life, faded. Was this what Jesus' love felt like? It was even better than walking to school with Debbie and Terrie, or sitting on Mom's lap way back when and hearing her sweet voice. This was love sweeter than anything.

For the first time since Mom got sick, I felt there was hope, and even though we continued to struggle, I never let go of it. The nails in Jesus' hands and feet had opened the box I was in, freeing me at last to become the person he and my friends knew I could be.

There have been many miracles in my life, yet the greatest, the one that made all the others possible, was the miracle of God's love, which he first brought home to me through the friendship of two girls named Terrie and Debbie.

Random
Acts of
Kindness

The Ups and Downs of a Yo-Yo Man

by Kevin D. Hendricks

"A street perfomer? Kevin, are you sure about this?" my mother asked.

"I'm good with my yo-yo tricks, Mom. I really think I can earn enough over the summer to survive."

I'd landed an internship in Chicago, working for a magazine publisher. It didn't pay anything, but they'd be putting me up for free in a college dorm room with an oven and a fridge. I only needed enough to pay my expenses—food, gas, and a social life.

Once you begin to acknowledge random acts of kindness—both the ones you have received and the ones you have given—you can no longer believe that what you do does not matter.

Dawna Markova

Mom wanted me to have a real job in the evenings to supplement my internship. And I tried. I filled out more applications than any person should have to, with no results. Doing yo-yo tricks on the street was my last hope. I *had* to try it.

Three days a week, I set up on the corner of Michigan Avenue and Pearson Street in downtown Chicago. I dressed in a

T-shirt and cargo shorts. I placed a plastic box labeled "College Student" in front of a CD player and played upbeat tunes. And my yo-yo danced.

Over and over, my shiny black yo-yo flew out in front of me, behind me, then back in front. With a flip of my wrist I let it "sleep," then I tossed it back on its string and made it "walk the tightrope." I moved as fast as I could to the music, keeping the yo-yo flying and the people watching.

A little kindness from person to person is better than a vast love for all humankind.
Richard Dehmel

As a street performer you have to be aware of who's watching. Your job is to make people passing by stop passing by. And once you have their attention, you have to continually wow them. I quickly learned that the longer they stood and watched, the more likely they were to drop change in my box.

High school kids emptied their pockets for me. A father handed his young child a dollar and the kid crawled forward to drop it in my box. My girlfriend's mother came to see me when she was in town for a visit and handed me a twenty. Those were good days.

But not everyone was kind. Some people made snide remarks. "That's what they teach you in college?" Junior high boys stared and announced, "I can do *that*." Then there were just the freeloaders. A lot of people just watched the entertainment, applauded my routine, and moved on—without leaving a dime. Usually the sidewalk sizzled with heat. Some days I felt it burning through my shoes, but I took few breaks and kept working the crowds. I had to earn. I couldn't let up.

One hot, humid day, a man watched me for quite a while. Finally, he introduced himself as Jay. "I've never seen anyone do that with a yo-yo," he said.

Kind words do not cost much. Yet they accomplish much.
BLAISE PASCAL

I threw the yo-yo straight up, then whipped it in all directions. "I've had a lot of practice," I told him, swinging a wide circle around my head. Sweat made my shirt cling to me, but I didn't stop trying to wow Jay. *This guy's going to leave a chunk of change.*

Jay watched for an hour or two, as if he had nothing else to do all afternoon. I got used to him being there. But once when I looked up, he had disappeared. I felt let down. Irked too. Jay was just another freeloader watching me work, contributing nothing. *What's wrong with people?*

I was still working hard when I heard a voice say, "Hey, man."

I stopped my yo-yo and turned to see Jay. He

held a brown paper sack. "You look thirsty." He pulled out two Cokes and handed me one.

I was *very* thirsty.

Jay pried off the metal bottle cap with his teeth, spit it in a trash can, and took a long swig. I went for my pocketknife.

Jay watched me struggle, then took my bottle, slipped the cap between his teeth, and lifted it off. He wiped the lip of the bottle with his shirt and handed it over. I raised the icy Coke and took a long, cold drink. I'd never tasted anything so good. "Thanks," I said.

He grinned. Revived, I tightened the yo-yo string on my finger and went back to work. Jay disappeared into the street. I never saw him again, yet I'll never forget him.

As perfume to the flower, so is kindness to speech.
Katherine Francke

Because of the generosity of strangers, I *was* able to survive on the money I made as a street performer that summer. And I discovered that whether it's pocket change or an icy-cold cola on a hot summer day, even the smallest act of kindness is something to cherish.

Be Mine

BY KATE HELGERMAN

My freshman year of high school was *not* going well. First my boyfriend dumped me. Then my best friend started dating my ex, and stopped speaking to me.

So when Valentine's Day rolled around, I was less than happy about it. All my friends had boyfriends or girlfriends or at least dates for that day. My big plans consisted of having dinner with my mom and grandma.

How far that little candle throws his beams! So shines a good deed in a weary world.
WILLIAM SHAKESPEARE

As we drove home that night, Mom asked how my Valentine's Day went. I started crying. "No one got me anything!"

When we got home, I went to my room. *Why is all this happening, God?* I prayed. *Please help me not to feel so alone!* After a while, I clicked on my computer and visited my favorite chat rooms. Even that didn't help. A couple hours later, Mom called me downstairs and handed me a plastic bag. "I found it hanging on the door. I guess someone left it for you."

What in the world . . . ? I opened the bag. Inside was a card with my name on it, a red rose, and a chocolate teddy bear lollipop. No signature. Was this God's answer to my prayer?

Always be a little kinder than necessary.
James M. Barrie

Mom swore she didn't send the gift, and she didn't act the slightest bit guilty. But even if she was my mystery "Valentine," I don't care. Because in that moment, I knew I was loved—by my mom and another special Someone!

Graduation Gift

by Lisa Maxbauer

I'm standing on my back patio, shaking my head. Dad has tied streamers and balloons to anything that's not moving. I walk over to a picnic table where a cake screams "Congratulations on your Graduation!" in gooey blue frosting.

Today is my graduation party. I consider it to be my last official duty as a person living under my parents' roof.

If you were busy being kind, Before you knew it, you would find You'd soon forget to think 'twas true That someone was unkind to you.

R. Foreman

"Lisa, time to get dressed! People will be here soon," Mom yells. "And don't even think about wearing those ratty blue jeans."

"Why not?" I yell back as I arrange paper napkins around the cake into rows of alternating blue and yellow. "They look fine!"

"You know, you could at least *pretend* that you'll miss us," my father jokes as he carries folding chairs out to the patio.

I march upstairs and change into a blue sundress. I keep my sneakers on. *In college I can wear whatever I want.*

• • •

I couldn't wait to leave for college. It's not that I didn't love my family. I just thought life around home was boring. Load the dishwasher every night. Go to church every Sunday. Help your sister with homework. I was ready for something new.

Even our holidays were always the same. Every winter, I had to help my mother bake cookies—hundreds of batches of cookies, all to be given away as holiday "care packages." Year after year, our kitchen became an assembly line. My mother mixed the batter, my little sister Jill arranged the cookies on wax paper to cool, and I put them in baggies and wrapped them in tissue paper and ribbons. So many gingerbread people, and none of them for us.

Don't wait for people to be friendly, show them how.
Author Unknown

When it was finally time to deliver the packages, Jill and I obediently zipped up our parkas and set out through the snow-covered streets.

Knock! Knock! Knock!

"Hi, Mrs. Whiteford. Here are some baked goods for your family from my family. Merry Christmas!"

My whole family piled into our brown station wagon to make deliveries to people who lived outside the neighborhood. We stopped at houses belonging to old people from church and long-lost friends of my parents. It seemed like every year, the list got longer.

One of the people on that list was a man who used to work at my father's hardware store. He lived alone in the smallest house I've ever seen. Other than that, I didn't really know anything about Rex. I didn't even know his last name. I never heard any mention of a wife or a family. But like clockwork every winter, my mother pulled into his driveway and my dad jogged to Rex's door to surrender the desserts. Then on to our next stop.

Have you had a kindness shown? Pass it on; 'twas not given for thee alone, pass it on; Let it travel down the years, let it wipe another's tears, till in heaven the deed appears, pass it on.

Henry Burton

I always complained. "Why do Jill and I have to come with you guys? We don't even know these people."

• • •

Back in my bedroom I can hear guests arriving. I make my way outside to greet people and claim my gifts. Like a swarm of bees, questions about my future start buzzing through the air.

"Think you'll be homesick out there in Indiana?" Uncle Paul says.

"Have you figured out what you're going to study at college?" Uncle Bill asks.

I smile politely and sip punch from my plastic glass.

Carry out a random act of kindness . . . someone somewhere might do the same for you.
Princess Diana

"Hey, your parents thought we should come over some night to watch your graduation video!" Uncle Chris says.

Oh, no. Not the video!

I circulate through the crowd. More people hug me and shake my hand.

"Your parents are sure going to miss you!" says Aunt Sue.

"Yeah, I'll miss them too."

But I am *really* looking forward to college. And I don't plan on coming home many weekends. Without much time off before Christmas, the cookie assembly line might have to function without me.

• • •

When I was young, Christmas seemed magical. Christmas Eve had always been my favorite. While the adults drank coffee and told boring stories, all of the young cousins waited for the main attraction. Finally, my grandfather would say, "I think I hear footsteps outside!"

Then, slowly, the front door would creak open. Santa had arrived—with a bag full of toys!

When we got older, we tried to discover Santa's true identity. But our list of suspects was too long. We could never tell which of the eight uncles was missing at the right moment.

"Uncle Paul, are you the Santa?" I guessed.

"Not me," he always laughed. "That's the real Santa."

Too often we underestimate the power of a touch, a smile, a kind word, a listening ear, an honest compliment, or the smallest act of caring, all of which have the potential to turn a life around.

LEO BUSCAGLIA

• • •

The party is in full swing. Cars line the street and the pile on the gift table grows taller by the minute. Without a place to park, a delivery truck stops in the middle of the road and a man jumps out carrying a package.

"Lisa, you'd better go get it. It's probably for you anyway," my father calls from across the yard.

The delivery man hands me a shoebox covered in brown paper. The return address: Rex Hanell.

Rex . . . Rex . . . Oh, it must be that old guy we used to deliver cookies to!

I can't remember the last time I've seen Rex. The package feels light in my hands. The shaky handwriting on the label looks almost foreign.

Suddenly, I feel an urge to open it. Glancing over my shoulder, I slip around the side of the house and tear open the wrapping. Inside is a stationary set with handmade paper and envelopes. *How nice of him.*

Then I open the card. It is black, with just one, short, handwritten message inside:

Good luck, from Santa.

P.S. Your folks probably never told you it was me.

The box slips out of my arms.

For a few seconds the party noises seem to disappear. I read the words again.

. . . it was me.

How beautiful a day can be when kindness touches it!

George Elliston

Rex was never a suspect in the ancient Santa mystery. Almost a decade had passed, but it made sense now. Without a family of his own, Rex would have been free on Christmas Eve. He probably loved his annual performance too. For years I had shared my family with him, without even knowing it.

Emerging from my hiding spot, I scan the congested backyard. All these people are here to see me. All of them have supported me, either visibly or invisibly, for years. *Why am I so eager to leave? Moving on to college shouldn't mean moving past my family.*

"I'm sure we'll miss her more than she'll miss us," I overheard my dad saying. "She's so independent. The house will be really quiet without her."

"Oh! Here's our guest of honor!" my mother calls, waving me toward them. "Lisa, everyone has been looking for you."

The more sympathy you give, the less you need.
Malcolm S. Forbes

"I'm right here." I give Mom a hug, still gripping the shoebox.

A piece of me will always be right here.

The Great Shoe Search

BY MARY KASTING

I have a date to the junior prom!

The big event was all my girlfriends and I had talked about at school. I pictured myself gliding across the dance floor in my pale blue gown, its skirt billowing around me as I twirled so light on my—

Boom! My fantasy crash-landed. I looked down at the end of the bed where my feet created a tall mound under the covers. Tomorrow I would have to find shoes. Matching my dress wasn't the problem. Fitting the canoes attached to my legs was.

I have always depended on the kindness of strangers.
TENNESSEE WILLIAMS

My feet were big. Too big. They were the most noticeable thing about me. I tripped over them when I walked, and classmates teased me about the skis sticking out from under my desk. Who was I kidding, thinking I would actually dance at the prom? I rolled over, envisioning Cinderella's wicked stepsisters trying to jam their ugly feet into her dainty glass slipper.

I woke up the next morning, rushed through breakfast, then dashed to the bus. I had made a list of the shoe stores in downtown Indianapolis, knowing I would probably have to visit every last one if I were to have any luck. Starting out on fashionable Washington Street, I worked my way down the list.

Finally, at a store near the bottom of the list, I made the same request I'd made all morning: "I'd like a pair of dressy heels, please."

"Of course," the salesman said. "What si—" Looking down at my feet, he quickly corrected himself. "I'm sorry. We don't carry your size."

The best portion of a good man's life is his little, nameless unremembered acts of kindness and of love.
William Wordsworth

I couldn't get out of there fast enough. What would I end up wearing, my brother's gym shoes? *God, can't you help me out?*

There was only one more place: Stout's Factory Shoe Store on Massachusetts Avenue—a business that had been around *forever*. I doubted it carried anything I would be interested in. But I was desperate.

Stout's yellowed window displayed "sensible" styles: crepe-soled nurses shoes, steel-toed work boots, white Keds. A bell tinkled as I opened the door and went in. The worn hardwood floor creaked under my clumsy steps. The air reeked of shoe polish.

"Hello! Hello!" came a raspy welcome. The bright-green parrot in a cage by the cash register had spied me. I was about to bolt when a short elderly man appeared at the back of the store. "Could I be of some service, young lady?" *How could this ancient man even imagine what a fifteen-year-old girl might need?*

"I don't suppose you have a pair of prom shoes to fit me," I said, pointing hopelessly at my feet.

The old man took me by the hand and led me to a chair. "Sit here," he said, bowing slightly, as if I were a princess. "I'll be back in a moment."

There is no beautifier of complexion, or form, or behavior, like the wish to scatter joy and not pain around us.
Ralph Waldo Emerson

What's he going to bring out? High-buttoned granny shoes? I thought. The parrot squawked in the background.

Finally the salesman returned with a box. He sat on a worn, sloped stool and deftly removed my shoes. Then he took a large pump from the box and slipped it onto my foot. "There now," he said. "Stand up and let's see about the fit."

I rose and nearly fell out of the pump. The old man steadied me on my feet. He had misjudged my size. The shoe was too big—*way* too big. That had never happened before. My foot was swimming in the pump he had brought out! Suddenly I felt deliriously happy.

The gentleman's eyes sparkled. "Oh, dear," he said. "Obviously these won't do. Let me get a smaller size." He scooped the reject back into the box and shuffled away.

A *smaller size*, I thought. The words sounded like music.

My elderly friend came back, barely visible behind the double stack of shoeboxes he juggled in his arms. "Perhaps we have something for you here."

I tried on pair after pair, in gold, pink, ivory, pearlized white. The salesman sat on his perch surrounded by a sea of open boxes, gently slipping my feet into one beautiful shoe after another. I told him about the prom, my date, my blue dress.

Give others a piece of your heart, not a piece of your mind.
Author Unknown

"Ahh," he said," in that case, let's try these." He swept aside the clutter of boxes and opened one from the bottom of his stack. Carefully he unwrapped the prettiest shoes I had seen all day: royal-blue satin heels. When he slipped them on my feet, I felt like Cinderella. A perfect fit! I wanted to get up and dance right there in the store.

"I'll wrap them for you," he said, looking pleased. While paying for my shoes, I wondered about his initial misjudgment. Could this experienced salesman honestly have been so wrong? Perhaps he knew more than just the business of shoes. . . .

Don't be yourself—be someone a little nicer.
MIGNON MCLAUGHLIN

As I left, the parrot squawked, "Good day." And it was, with a little help from a wise salesman in an old store, where my own two feet—and God—had taken me.

The Twelve-Day Conspiracy

By Melanie Petersen

"What a Christmas season," I complained. "It's only the first week of December, and I'm already stressed out. I'm broke and tired, and tinsel and Christmas carols just aren't doing anything for me this year."

Practice random kindness and senseless acts of beauty.
Anne Herbert

My friend Lori laughed and agreed. Together we lay on my bed and complained about our holiday blues. We reminisced about childhood Christmases when school pageants and Santa's approaching visit were enough to spark the Christmas magic. But what do you do to bring back that special holiday feeling when you're seventeen years old?

We pondered that thought and after some brainstorming came up with a plan. The more we talked about it and the more ideas I scribbled down on my notepad, the more excited we became. Lori and I decided to be Santa for someone else. We decided to give "The Twelve Days of Christmas" anonymously to a person we felt needed some holiday cheer more than we did.

We looked around school the next day, hoping to find the perfect person to receive our Christmas cheer. It was after psychology class when Lori ran up to me in the hall. "I know who," she said, smiling.

Brad was a boy in our class no one really knew. He was shy and didn't smile much. Lori talked to his friend Ryan and discovered that Brad's parents were ill, so he spent most of his time working to provide money for his family. He was on the wrestling team, and Ryan said that was all Brad had time for.

We cannot hold a torch to light another's path without brightening our own.

Ben Sweetland

Before we knew it, December 12 came. With our first gift and poem ready, we jumped in the car and made our way to Brad's house out in the country.

"Turn off your lights," Lori warned. We parked the car down the dirt road from his house and began our trek to his front door. My heart was beating fast. I was excited, and a little frightened of getting caught.

Our first poem read:

On the first day of Christmas
We're bringing you some treats.
We'll be bringing something for the next twelve days,
Because we think you're neat.

Love,
Santa's Elves

Lori and I tucked it into the package on Brad's doorstep, rang the doorbell, and then ran back to the car as fast as we could.

Every night our expedition became a little more difficult but a lot more fun. The second night Brad's friend Ryan showed up at Lori's front door with another friend, Damon, and a plateful of fudge. "We made this fudge," he said. "Can we come too?" I was impressed.

Goodness is achieved not in a vacuum, but in the company of other men, attended by love.
SAUL BELLOW

Before our project was completed, our parents, Lori's neighbor, and several others asked to share in our project. My dad came into my room and handed me a gift certificate to a clothing store in town. "I'd like you to give this to him on the last night," he said. Lori's neighbor gave us a beautiful gift-boxed tie, and her parents loaned us their car when we thought Brad might recognize mine. One night my fourteen-year-old brother handed me some money to help with the presents and swallowed his cool image long enough to ask if he could come along on the last night. Christmas was looking brighter and brighter.

At school the day before the Christmas break, the wrestlers had an assembly. Lori and I watched for Brad, and when he walked out on stage with the other athletes, we noticed he was wearing two new things: a big smile and the tie we had left him the night before.

The final night, we loaded our gift box with lots of things: the gift certificate, a ham for his family, cookies, and other treats. As we made our way down the country road for the last time, I silently reflected on the fact that Christmas had never been quite so meaningful to me. Never in all the years of waiting for Santa had I ever felt this good. We all sang Christmas carols on the way home, feeling a special bond of friendship.

Do unto others as you would have them do unto you.
Luke 6:31

We don't think Brad has ever discovered who the elves were, and we hope he never does. Most important, I hope we never forget that special feeling we get inside when we are giving true Christlike love at Christmas—and all year through.

The Book Lady

BY TERRY A. ZIER

Fluffing up the pillow beneath my head, I sighed and stared at the ceiling. The room was silent but for my breathing. I turned my head toward the door. No one would venture down this deserted hospital hallway. Except for my parents, I hadn't had any visitors since being admitted, because my doctor didn't yet know what was wrong with me. I had been far too tired for a normal thirteen-year-old, and was having trouble digesting my food. Some days I was almost too weak to walk, but there seemed to be no medical explanation for my condition.

An anxious heart weighs a man down, but a kind word cheers him up.
PROVERBS 12:25

Tears stung my eyes. I was tired of having no one to talk to. A roommate was out of the question. The quarantine sign on my door meant even the nuns steered clear. *What can I do stuck alone in this room?* Then a knock came at the door.

It swung open and a woman stepped in, pulling a cart behind her. Her uniform told me she was a candy striper, but she was middle-aged, not a teenager. She smiled at me warmly, and I found myself smiling back. "Call me the book lady," she announced, coming right up to my bed and holding out her hand. I started. Hadn't she seen the sign on my door?

"It's all right," she said, "I understand." She patted my shoulder. "Now, let's see what goodies we have in here." She turned to her cart. I could feel a lump rising in my throat. I wasn't a great reader.

"Here," she said, handing me a slim hardcover. "What about *Rebecca of Sunnybrook Farm?*" I bit my lip. "What's wrong?" the lady asked. "It's hard for me to read," I admitted, shame turning my stomach to jelly. The book lady sat at the edge of my bed. "What better time to improve your reading than now?" she asked. "Are you scared?" I nodded. "That's okay. Everybody gets scared sometimes."

You cannot do a kindness too soon, for you never know how soon it will be too late.

Ralph Waldo Emerson

"The doctor doesn't know what's wrong with me," I said, fiddling with the bedspread. "And nobody comes to visit because I might make them sick. I wish I had someone to talk to."

The book lady tilted her head and looked at

me. "You can always talk to God. He wants you to. And he always listens. That's why he's there." I had never really heard much about God before.

"He'll listen to me when I'm sad?" I asked, wanting to make sure. Maybe I didn't have to feel so lonely.

"Of course," the book lady said. "Especially when you're sad." She rose and straightened her red-and-white-striped smock. "I'll come by day after tomorrow," she promised. "So start reading *Rebecca* and we'll talk about it then." Flashing me another smile, she gripped the handle of her cart and started out of my room.

This world is but the vestibule of eternity. Every good thought or deed touches a chord that vibrates in heaven.
Author Unknown

"What's your name?" I asked. She stopped for a minute and looked at me kindly. "Like I said, you can call me the book lady. Bye-bye." I waved, and then she and her cart were gone. I fingered the frayed binding of *Rebecca*. The book lady was right. This was the perfect time to work on my reading. Flipping to the first page, I began chapter one.

Two days later, as promised, the book lady came back.

"How are you liking the story?" she asked, coming close to me as she had the first time.

"Very much, thank you," I said, suddenly shy. "I've been reading a lot."

Fluffing her bobbed hair, the lady nodded. "That's good." She held out another book. "It's the next in the collection. I think you'll really enjoy it."

A shiver of anticipation ran through me when I took the next *Rebecca* book in my hands. "Thank you," I replied, lying back on my pillow.

"Rest now," the lady said. "I'll see you day after tomorrow."

All that day and the next I read my books and talked to God. *Thank you for sending me a friend*, I said. *And please help the doctor find out what's wrong with me so I can go home soon*. I felt a lot better when I talked to God.

The way to develop the best that is in a man is by appreciation and encouragement.
Charles Schwab

Every other morning for a month and a half the lady visited me, introducing me to countless friends in the books she brought.

Then one morning, after the nurse had taken my breakfast tray, my doctor came in. "Terry," he said, "we're sending you home this morning. Whatever was ailing you seems to have gone away."

Home! The doctor said my father was waiting for me in the lobby. I dressed and went down with the nurse in the elevator. "How are you, missy?" Dad asked.

"Glad to be leaving the hospital!" I said, grinning. He took my hand.

"Wait!" I had almost forgotten my friend. "I want to say good-bye to the book lady." The nurse looked at me curiously. "Is she working today?" I asked.

Do it that very moment! Don't put it off—don't wait. There's no use in doing a kindness If you do it a day too late!
CHARLES KINGSLEY

"What book lady?" my doctor wondered.

"The book lady," I insisted. "In a candy-striper uniform. She came by my room every other day while I was here."

The nurse shook her head. "We haven't had a book volunteer for a long time," she said.

"But she visited me. . . ." My voice trailed off. The doctor and nurse eyed me suspiciously, as if worried they'd released me too soon.

"Come on, Terry," my dad said. "Let's go."

"Bye, now," called the nurse. "Take care," called the doctor. Dad and I walked out into the sun toward the car. I knew there had been a book lady—she might not have worked for the hospital, but she did work for God.

"Can we stop at the library?" I asked my father. "I have some new friends waiting there."

My heart is always happy when I truthfully can say that by the grace of God I made another friend today.

James J. Metcalfe

Kindness
to the
Rescue

Running Late

By Tara Holt

"Josh, hurry! I have basketball practice before school. If you want a ride, get out of the bathroom *now*!"

"Okay, okay. I'm ready. Let's roll." Josh emerged from the bathroom, slapping gel on his hair.

We ran to the Jeep, our breath leaving white puffs in the November air. Josh cranked up the heat, then rubbed his hands together.

The everyday kindness of the back roads more than makes up for the acts of greed in the headlines.
Charles Kuralt

"This is happening way too much," I said as we turned onto the road. "I'm going to get in trouble with my coach. When you have practice, I always get you to school on time."

"In two years, I'll be old enough to drive myself," said Josh. "I can't wait."

I wouldn't admit it to my little brother, especially today, but I really did enjoy his company. We had a lot in common, like playing and watching baseball. When we had a free night and the Braves were on, we always watched together. But when it came to getting Josh moving in the morning . . . well, sometimes he just got on my nerves.

The heater slowly kicked in as the Jeep bumped along our country road. Only eight miles to school—we'd be there in just a few minutes.

A low, long train whistle sounded in the distance. Josh looked at me. "It's early for the train."

If you stop to be kind, you must swerve often from your path.
Mary Webb

He was right. We hardly ever saw a train in the mornings, even when we were running late.

"Go fast, we can beat it!" Josh pleaded.

I stepped on the gas. Trees lining the road turned to green streaks. As the tracks came into view, the approaching train neared. But I'd never been a huge risk-taker. I wasn't about to take a chance and run into tons of bone-crushing metal. I slowed down.

"Do a U-turn. Let's try a different road," said Josh. "We can get ahead of it."

I took Josh's advice. We left a trail of dust behind us as we sped to another crossing.

About a mile down the road, Josh yelled, "Tara, look!"

"What?"

"In the water . . . pickup truck. And look—

there's a *man* in there!" Before I could even stop completely, Josh leapt from the Jeep. I pulled over, grabbed my cell phone, and ran after him toward an overflowing drainage ditch. He kicked off his shoes and jumped from the steep embankment into the water.

Beginning today, treat everyone you meet as if they were going to be dead by midnight. Extend to them all the care, kindness, and understanding you can muster, and do it with no thought of any reward. Your life will never be the same again.
Og Mandino

I dialed 911 as Josh swam toward the man. The guy looked dazed, just standing there in chest-high water, near his truck.

"911. What's your emergency?"

"There's a wreck. . . ." I stammered.

"Where are you?" the 911 lady asked.

"Uh . . . I don't know the name of this dirt road! My brother just jumped into the water. There's a man in there. His truck must have gone off the road, right into the water."

I had to focus and give solid directions, but my heart was with Josh swimming toward the man. That water had to be *freezing.*

"One mile south of South Coffeyville," I blurted. "We're on a dirt road near a railroad crossing." She asked about the man in the water as Josh continued to wade toward him.

"Are you okay?" Josh yelled. "Can you come to me?"

The man mumbled something. Then he stumbled, falling face-first into the water.

Oh God, I prayed. *Please don't let him die.*

"I'm not sure how hurt the man is, but he just slipped under the water," I told the dispatcher.

Josh grabbed him by the back of his shirt and pulled his face above water. Then Josh started dragging him toward the bank. The man began to struggle. *Good,* I thought. *At least he's alive.* He tried to pull away, but Josh held onto him. Blood was running down the poor guy's face.

Nothing makes one feel so strong as a call for help.
George MacDonald

"I'll never get him out of the water," Josh yelled. "The bank is too steep!"

I knew there was no way I could pull him out, either. "It's okay. The 911 dispatcher says to keep him still. Help is on the way." I hung up the phone.

Oh please, God, protect Josh from the cold. And don't let that man die.

Josh shivered. It was all he could do to keep the man's bloody head from slipping under the water. "Tara, he's still breathing. But barely."

The man groaned, slipping in and out of consciousness. "Someone will be here soon," I kept telling Josh. "Keep his neck still. Hang in there."

I looked at Josh in that freezing water. Only twenty minutes ago, I'd been upset with him for making us late. Now, I couldn't be more proud of my little brother.

A good character is the best tombstone. Those who loved you and were helped by you will remember you when forget-me-nots have withered. Carve your name on hearts, not on marble.
Charles H. Spurgeon

Finally, I heard sirens. A police car pulled up, followed by a fire truck. Two firemen ran down the ditch and trudged into the water to help Josh. The ambulance arrived moments later.

I stepped back and watched the EMTs take control. It took several rescuers to lift the man from the water and load him onto a stretcher and into an ambulance. "You okay, son?" one of the rescue workers asked Josh.

"Yeah, just cold," he answered, teeth chattering.

"You'd better get yourself checked out by a doctor," a paramedic said. "And get out of those wet clothes!"

It wasn't until the rescue vehicles drove off that

I realized for the first time how scared I really was. I wiped my tears on my sleeve and hugged Josh. I didn't even mind that he was soaked and filthy.

"You were great," I said.

"Yeah, you were pretty great yourself," he said. "I guess we were late this morning for a reason. . . ."

"Okay, hero," I said. "Let's get you home to change."

He who sees a need and waits to be asked for help is as unkind as if he had refused it.

Dante Alighieri

Duck Rescue

BY ADRIAN CRAWFORD

It was a Sunday afternoon—Mother's Day—and my friend Adam and I were splashing through puddles on our way home from Walgreens. I'd just picked out the perfect (last minute!) Mother's Day gift, a beautiful red rose. "Mom will love this," I told Adam. What mother doesn't love roses?

As we rounded a corner and started down an alley, we saw a strange sight: a duck. Make that a crazy duck, squawking and flapping her wings, running around in the middle of the road near a sewer drain. "Check it out!" Adam said, as he peered through the drain cover. There were *more* ducks down there. Little ones, all piled on top of each other.

Those who bring sunshine into the lives of others, cannot keep it from themselves.
JAMES M. BARRIE

"How do you think they got down there?" Adam said.

"I have no idea, but they look cold and scared." The mother duck kept squawking. "We have to get them out!" I said.

I laid Mom's rose at the side of the road, and we

pried off the metal grate. Adam and I took turns holding each other's ankles while we fished twelve baby ducks from the four-foot hole. It wasn't easy, especially since it had started to drizzle again. But it was worth it to see the ducklings, all wet and scraggly, squeezing close to their mom.

Afterward, Adam and I were soaked and muddy. Mom's rose took a beating too. It wasn't ruined, but it sure wasn't perfect anymore. So much for my Mother's Day gift.

Later, Mom told me she didn't mind one bit about her soggy, last-minute rose. Turns out she thought my "rescue mission" was the best Mother's Day present ever. I guess that mother duck probably did too!

He was so benevolent, so merciful a man that he would have held an umbrella over a duck in a shower of rain.

Douglas William Jerrold

The Trials of Leaping Lizard

BY LARRY L. SHORT

All the way up the mountain to the camp I managed to keep my fears in the back of my mind. Only when I was standing in the mud in a tattered, eight-man teepee did I begin to have second thoughts about the whole thing. Here I was, a first-year counselor for a junior summer camp in Southern California. And I was surrounded by eight pale-faced little Indians, all listening to the rain splattering on the canvas.

Kind words toward those you daily meet, Kind words and actions right, Will make this life of ours most sweet, Turn darkness into light.

ISAAC WATTS

I was really nervous because of a problem I've always had. Some people say I'm accident-prone—I really don't know what to call it. Maybe I'm just clumsy. But as long as I can remember, I've been falling from trikes, bikes, skates, walls, ladders, trees, and horses. I am constantly colliding with stationary objects, stepping on nails, banging my head, or cutting myself. Once I even shot myself in the foot with an arrow. So, not knowing what "accidents" the summer would bring, I felt uneasy.

Since the teepee only held eight and I was the ninth man, I slept outside the first night. I managed to get one hour of sleep before I had to go off to a staff meeting at 6:30 A.M., during which we were informed that recent rains had brought out swarms of scorpions. So in addition to all our other staff duties, every morning and night we were to check bags, clothing, shoes, and suitcases for the creatures. But we weren't to let the kids know what we were checking them for.

The heart benevolent and kind the most resembles God.
ROBERT BURNS

My Indians were the wildest, rowdiest, stubbornest bunch of boys I had ever seen. And they were mine for seven days. During the course of the week, I suffered my usual mishaps. I was gashed by a thornbush while hiding from sneaky campers seeking vengeance with water balloons. I wrenched my shoulder and bruised my knee during some inhumane game I'd prefer not to think about. And then, to top everything off, I came down with a bad cold. Worst of all, though, was my emotional condition. By the second day, I was frustrated and exhausted. *Why, Lord, why? Why pick on me?*

Then, at least in my own mind, even the other counselors began turning against me. They teased me constantly about a girl counselor I had thought I was successfully managing to keep away from. I would even interpret remarks meant to encourage me as being sarcastic and mean.

Then the unthinkable happened. During a fast and furious volleyball game, and with a day and a night still left to go, my glasses—thick, wire-rimmed ones I can barely see without—were knocked flying from my face. The ominous crash and tinkle of broken glass announced the news before observers had time to tell me. My glasses, so essential to my daily existence, were broken. And I had no extra pair.

Life is made up, not of great sacrifices or duties, but of little things, in which smiles and kindness and small obligations win and preserve the heart.
Humphrey Davy

Full of despair, I picked up the pieces and started feeling my nearsighted way toward the administrator's office. My panicked thoughts, centering mainly around the remaining time I had left to counsel my little tribe, were suddenly interrupted by a Bible verse that popped into my mind: "In everything give thanks. . . ." (1 Thessalonians 5:18). Somehow, something compelled me to say, honestly, "Thank you, Lord." I'd never done that before, but the clouds of despair lifted and the Lord seemed to say, "Don't worry. Everything will be all right."

That evening, my Indians held a private powwow and then made a solemn announcement, addressing me by my Indian name.

"Leaping Lizard, we took a vote and decided we're going to be your slaves and your eyes for the rest of the week."

From that moment on, my time at junior camp was spent in peaceful bliss as I was led around by my young Indians who heeded my every word. Then, right before I left, another counselor handed me a wad of bills to pay for my glasses. They had taken up a collection for me. I almost cried.

Forget injuries. Never forget kindesses.

Chinese Proverb

As I was leaving the camp, I turned around and thought, *Wow, Lord, these guys really did love me after all!* Through them I found that if I am thankful when a mishap occurs, the Lord will give me something to be thankful for later. And that's good news for a klutz like me!

Ginger's Hope

By Chris Gesner

The minute I met Ginger, I could tell right away that she was a dog that didn't trust anyone. She didn't want to be touched. She flinched if anybody reached out to her too quickly. She huddled in a corner by herself, shutting the whole world out. This is how abused animals act.

Ginger's such a sweet dog, I can't imagine why anybody would have abused her. But people are just mean sometimes, and they don't care if they hurt you. No matter how much wrong they do, they think their actions are justified. I know firsthand, because my stepfather abused me.

Kindness is the ability to love someone more than they deserve.
Author Unknown

It started when I was seven. He'd get angry, then beat me with his fist or belt buckle or whatever was handy. He threw me around a lot, and once he even pulled a gun on me. He treated my mom the same way. I was too young to do anything about it, so I looked for ways to escape. Mostly, I hung out with a neighbor kid who was a few years older than me, and we smoked pot. It made me feel better—for a little while, anyway.

My stepfather got really sick and almost died when I was nine. While he was in the hospital, my mom decided it was a good time for us to escape the abuse. She got us a place to live where he couldn't find us. But by then, the damage had been done. I was full of anger. I started acting tough so nobody would mess with me.

By the time I was thirteen, I was getting into trouble with the law, not going to school, that sort of thing. When I was fifteen, I was put into a group home, but I hated it there. I ran away after a month. Finally, I contacted my real dad, and he let me move in with him. But my anger was still out of control. One day at school, I beat up a kid pretty bad. Something inside me exploded. I stole his money and ran.

Kindness is the noblest weapon to conquer with.
American Proverb

I was arrested. At first, I didn't think it was any big deal—I was only seventeen, so I was still a minor. Plus, the kid I beat up was going to be okay, and I didn't have a history of violent crime. Even when my lawyer told me about a strict mandatory sentencing law for juveniles in Oregon, I didn't worry that much about it.

So when the judge sentenced me to five years and ten months at MacLaren Juvenile Correctional

Facility, I was stunned. *This is like something on TV,* I thought. *It can't be happening!*

I got to MacLaren in June, 1999. Fences surrounded the campus, which was made up of low, sandy brick buildings and huge, tent-like structures. Each building and tent was fenced in too. Fences inside of fences. Locks inside of locks. As we drove through the front gate, I looked down at my handcuffs and shackles. *I'm going to be locked up here until I'm almost twenty-four!* I thought. *How am I going to survive?*

The first place I went was the intake unit. They didn't do a whole lot to make me feel welcome. To them, I was just another kid gone wrong. They weren't interested that I was sentenced for the only violent crime I'd committed. I was sentenced for violence, and that made me dangerous.

Kindness is like a rose, which though easily crushed and fragile, yet speaks a language of silent power.
Francis J. Roberts

I was held in the intake unit, in a room by myself, for a couple of days. Then I was released to live in one of the huge tents. I soon found out that they called the fenced area around the tent "the cage." And that's what I felt like—an animal in a cage.

A few days after I'd been put in there, I remembered something my mom had told me after I'd been sentenced. She'd read on the Internet that some of the guys at MacLaren were training homeless dogs. I'd always loved dogs, so I started asking around to see what I could find out about the program.

"Yeah, it's called Project Pooch," one of the guys told me. "You get to help train abused dogs so they can be adopted. But you have to apply for the program. They don't take just anybody."

I just have to get involved in that program, I told myself. *It's the only way I'll make it in this place.* I sure wasn't going to get close to any human in here. But a dog—you can count on a dog. Treat a dog right, and he loves you every time.

One day when I was out in the cage, someone pointed out Joan Dalton to me. "That's the woman you need to talk to about the dogs. " I asked permission to walk to the front of the cage so I could talk to her.

You can accomplish by kindness what you cannot do by force.

Publilius Syrus

One of the guys who knew Ms. Dalton stood there with me and called her over. "This is Chris," he told her. "He's interested in Project Pooch."

She didn't exactly smile, but she looked friendly. I cleared my throat. "I love dogs," I told her. "I'd really love to be in your program." She looked me in the eye. "It takes more than loving dogs," she said.

"You have to make a commitment. At least eight hours a day, five days a week. Your dogs come before anything else happening on campus. That means cleaning up after them, grooming them, training them, feeding them. They'll depend on you."

"I'll be able to do that," I told her. "I'm a good worker. I'll do whatever I need to."

She hesitated for a minute, still holding my gaze. "Okay," she said, finally. "I'll send you an application. You fill it out and we'll take it from there. You'll have to get security clearance too. We can't take a chance on anyone hurting a dog."

There is a grace of kind listening, as well as a grace of kind speaking.

Frederick William Faber

A few days passed, and I started to worry that Ms. Dalton had forgotten about me. *Maybe I made a bad impression on her,* I thought. *Maybe I won't qualify because of my past.* As last, I received the application. I filled it out, and a couple of weeks later I was invited to come for an interview with Ms. Dalton and the other guys who worked with Pooch. Nobody gave away what they were thinking during the interview, but by the end of the day, I got the news I made it. I was so relieved!

My first dog was a German shepherd named Duke. He had been neglected, and he came to us from the Humane Society. It felt great to have a dog in my life! Duke was always happy to see me, wagging his tail and barking. I'd been alone for so long. Duke was like a miracle.

When Duke was adopted by a family six weeks later, I thought I'd fall completely apart. Saying good-bye was very emotional. I even cried, something I hadn't done since I was a little kid.

Be kind to unkind people—they need it the most.
Author Unknown

I didn't have long to dwell on missing Duke, though. Right after he left, I got a new dog—Ginger, an English pointer. She's the one that was abused by her former owner. And boy, was she a challenge.

When Ms. Dalton introduced me to her, she was crouched in a corner with her tail between her legs, shaking like crazy. "Here, Ginger!" I held out my hand, and moved a little closer to her.

Ginger turned her sad eyes away and shook even harder. She didn't even know what kindess was. "I know how it is, Ginger," I told her. "We'll just go slow."

Every day for weeks, I went through the same routine with her. I'd sit about three feet away and talk to her. She wouldn't look at me, she'd just tremble in fear. Gradually, she got a little curious and would sniff, like she wanted to know more about me. But when I'd hold my hand out to her, she'd back away and shake again. We went through this several times every day. But I was patient. I knew what her fear was like. I hadn't let anybody close to me, either. Once you suffer abuse, you learn not to trust again. Trusting can lead to more pain.

Even when I wasn't with Ginger, I thought about her. *How can I get through to her? How can I let her know that I'm her friend, that everybody's not out to hurt her?* Sometimes I thought it'd be just impossible.

But I didn't give up. Little by little, I showed her I was her friend. I talked to her in a real soft voice. I made slow movements. Every time she made even a little bit of progress, I rewarded her with treats. I always told her what a good dog she was and how beautiful she was. Slowly, the shaking stopped. But she still wouldn't come close.

Constant kindness can accomplish much. As the sun makes ice melt, kindness causes misunderstanding, mistrust, and hostility to evaporate.
Albert Schweitzer

Then one day, when I reached out to her, she came near me. She looked me in the eyes and she wagged her tail. It was like opening a Christmas present I'd waited for all my life.

And a second gift was this:

while Ginger was learning to trust me, I was learning to trust too. And I didn't even realize it. The first person I trusted was Richard, the man who manages Project Pooch. One day, he called me aside and told me he was glad I was there. He told me he respected me because I put the dogs first. It was one of the first compliments I'd received in my life, and I could tell by his expression that he was speaking from his heart. *This guy sees me for who I am*, I thought. *He's not going to turn on me*.

I went over to Ginger and scratched her behind the ears. *If she can trust people after all she's been through, then I can too*.

Kind words are the music of the world.

Frederick William Faber

A couple months later, Ginger was adopted. It was tough seeing her go, but for some reason it wasn't as hard as it had been with Duke. Sure, I was sad. But mixed in with that were feelings of pride and hope. Ginger had learned to trust in human kindness again. She was healed. And so was I.

Fire and Rescue

by Ben Womick

I was fifteen and angry about everything. Then came my grandfather's accident.

3:30 A.M., December 26. The flaming house smelled like soggy burnt toast, sulfur, and oily car exhaust.

"On your left, Ben! Kitchen curtains!" Steve shouted, his voice muffled behind his oxygen mask.

I angled the nozzle of the heavy rubber hose toward the far wall and slowly twisted the pressure release valve. Denny, another firefighter, and I braced ourselves for the backward kick that would slam us off our feet if we weren't ready.

We do the works, but God works in us the doing of the works.

Saint Augustine of Hippo

There should have been a rumbling, teeth-rattling *whoosh* like a freight train, followed by pulse-whacks of water strong enough to punch holes in the wall. Instead, we got little more than a trickle. The water line was frozen.

"Line's blocked, Steve," I yelled, backing toward the door. "Denny, move out." We'd done all we could before the water lines froze.

The flames took a couple of hours to die down. As soon as it was safe, we started salvaging anything we could from the smoldering ruins. There wasn't much.

Sometimes a fire plays strange pranks. It'll twist itself like a tornado through corners and hideaways, but spare something completely unexpected. It was that way with this blaze: A stack of soggy but otherwise unharmed Christmas presents that had just been opened lay safe on the floor of a bedroom closet. Most of the furniture and valuables in the house were a total loss, but the contents of that one closet looked fine.

My partners helped me carry everything from the closet out to the front yard, where the stunned family started sifting through the meager pile.

"I wish we could've saved more," I mumbled, feeling really sorry for them.

"It's okay," the woman responded. She looked down at her two small children. "You rescued everything I care about. I'll be thanking you every day for the rest of my life."

Life is mostly froth and bubble, Two things stand like stone—Kindness in another's trouble, Courage in your own.
Adam L. Gordon

Her words took me back a year and a half, when I was fifteen and nobody's hero. I was running with the wrong crowd, cutting classes, staying out past curfew, and then arguing about it with my mother—all for no real reason. Homework? I didn't do it. My grades plummeted. Chores? Forget it. I spent more time making up excuses than it would have taken me just to do everything. Go to church? No way. Church was boring.

My parents reacted the way all parents probably do: lectures, endless "for your own good" and "you'll never get into a good college" speeches, and the taking away of my privileges. I yelled, slammed doors, talked back, and said a lot of things I felt sorry about later.

The only person I really cared much about was my grandfather. And then something awful happened to him.

He who wants to do good knocks at the gate: he who loves finds the door open.

Rabrindranath Tagore

My cousin, Jamie, and I were helping him clear brush from the back of his lot one summer day, and Grandpa wanted to smoke out some bees that had built a hive in an old rotted-out log. He got a small can of gasoline from the garage, poured it over the timber, then straightened up to light a match.

All of a sudden we heard this loud, explosive *POP*. In an instant a ball of hot flames flashed from the fuel-soaked wood and streaked up Grandpa's overalls. Screaming, he fell to the ground and started rolling across the grass.

"Get the hose, Jamie!" I yelled, grabbing an

old tarp as I sprinted across the lawn. "Grandma! Call 911!"

The ambulance attendants told us that third-degree burns covered over fifty percent of Grandpa's body. The surgeons at the regional burn center in Charleston, North Carolina, did what they could, cutting away charred areas and grafting on new skin. But when I visited him—at least twice a week—I kept wondering if there wasn't something more I could have done to save him. Maybe if I'd been paying closer attention. . . .

Any man's life will be filled with constant and unexpected encouragement if he makes up his mind to do his level best each day.
Booker T. Washington

I could tell Grandpa was in a lot of pain. He never talked about it, though. He never talked about anything except the fishing trip we'd take when he got home. And about how lucky he felt because God had spared his life. That made me mad. If God cared so much, why had the accident happened in the first place? All Grandpa said when I asked that was, "Sometimes God works in mysterious ways, Ben."

In September, after three long months in the burn center, Grandpa came home. The burns weren't healing the way they would on a younger man, and he was in a lot of pain. *What can I do to make him better?* I asked myself. *How can I make things like they were before?* We still talked about going fishing, but I realized it probably wouldn't happen. Most afternoons he sat in an old wooden rocker out on the back porch, reading the newspaper and visiting with anybody who came by to take his mind off of his discomfort. Once a week or so I'd pick up a couple pints of ice cream and drive over there after school to visit. *Maybe he'll be stronger today*, I'd think. *I've got his favorite flavor. . . .*

One afternoon, I found Steve, an old friend of the family, already there visiting. While the three of us sat on the porch eating ice cream, Grandpa said, "Steve's telling me about how he's volunteering for the fire department."

Note how good you feel after you have encouraged someone else. No other argument is necessary to suggest that you never miss the opportunity to give encouragement.
George Adams

The fire department was the last thing I wanted to hear about. I hadn't so much as lit a match since Grandpa's accident.

Steve said, "One of the guys invited me to a meeting a couple of months ago. It sounded interesting, so I signed up. It's really helped me get myself together and figure out my priorities." He looked over at me. "You should come to a meeting sometime. I think you'd like it."

"Not me." I dug into my ice cream. The raspy creak of Grandpa's rocker came to a halt as he nudged me with his foot.

"Sounds like a good program down there. Why don't you go check it out, Ben?"

"Aw, I don't know."

Grandpa put a hand on my shoulder. "Just think about it."

I did. Actually, I tried not to, but somehow the idea wouldn't go away.

Grandpa struggled, but he didn't make it through that winter. The burns on his legs wouldn't heal, and his heart was in poor shape. His death really shook me. I'd always been close to my grandfather, and somehow I'd assumed that he'd always be there for me. Everything around me was a mess—school, church, my relationship with my parents, the friends I hung out with. The only thing I hadn't destroyed was the relationship I had with Grandpa. Now he wasn't going to be around. Something had to change. *I* had to change. I just wasn't sure how.

If you have not often felt the joy of doing a kind act, you have neglected much, and most of all yourself.

A. Neilen

Then I remembered Steve and the fire department and how much Grandpa had wanted me to try it. So I signed up.

The older guys were skeptical about a sixteen-year-old sticking with the program, but I kept showing up for every fire and rescue class the county offered. When training was finished, I hung out at the firehouse. It took three months before I was allowed to do much more than get stuff off of the truck, but eventually the chief called me in, handed me a pager, and signed me on as third man on a three-man crew.

My first emergency call wasn't even a fire. An elderly woman had been cooking dinner for her grandkids. One minute she was standing in front of the stove; the next, she'd fallen over unconscious.

"She's in full cardiac arrest. Ben, get the kit," my crew chief, Denny, instructed when we found her. He started CPR.

Not one of us knows what effect his life produces, and what he gives to others; that is hidden from us and must remain so.
Albert Schweitzer

I watched, remembering my training classes. *This is the real thing!* Denny looked up at me. "Ben, take over here so I can get the meds going."

Me? I felt my heart thud. But I knelt and I put my hands lightly over his, absorbing and then assuming his cadence. The woman, dressed in a cotton apron and a flowered housedress, reminded me of a fragile bird.

"One, two, three," I counted. Everything else in the small kitchen blurred as my training took over. *Come on, breathe*. Between counts, I found myself praying, *Don't let her die, God*. It was the first prayer I'd uttered since before Grandpa's accident.

"We've got a pulse!" Denny shouted.

Three endless minutes later, the ambulance pulled up outside. It's customary for the person administering CPR on site to work the patient all the way to the hospital, so I kept on counting—and praying—as the techs wheeled us out on the gurney. Mike and Dan followed in the truck. At the hospital, the woman was rushed into the ER.

Kindness is love in work clothes.
Author Unknown

My job was finished, but I felt as if a train had run over me. I looked around the emergency room lobby. The last time I'd been there was three months before, the night my grandpa died of heart failure. I'd been mad at the world. Mad at my parents for no good reason. Mad at God too. Then I remembered what Grandpa had said about God using bad circumstances for good. I'd kept a woman's heart beating until she could get to a doctor! Maybe Grandpa had been right. I might never have been here helping to save a life if it hadn't been for Grandpa's accident.

Denny touched my shoulder. "Good job, Ben. I think she's gonna make it."

A month later, Edith Ziegler walked into the fire station. Mrs. Ziegler looked nothing like the desperately ill woman we'd left at the emergency room. I'd never seen a more beautiful sight in my life than that eighty-one-year-old lady standing at the end of that empty truck bay. She came up to me carrying a foil-covered platter. "I want to thank you boys for rescuing me from certain death." She smiled. "I made you all a big batch of chocolate chip cookies."

Great persons are able to do great kindnesses.
Miguel de Cervantes

I took the platter and told her thank you.

She peered at the brass name badge above the pocket of my shirt. "Are you a relation of Romeo Womick?"

"He was my grandfather."

She nodded. "Thought so. He was a kind man. Anyone ever tell you you're just like your grandpa? You are, you know. You surely are."

A knot of emotion stuck in my throat. She couldn't have paid me a bigger compliment. Maybe I had rescued her. But God had rescued me. And Grandpa had known just what I'd needed all along.

Escape from Gakowa

BY KATHERINE FLOTZ

We all knew what would happen if the Russian soldiers caught us sneaking through the cornfield. They would return us to camp and imprison us for days in a cellar, with no light, no food, and no toilet. They'd torture us. They might even leave us to die. Still, we had to try to escape.

Cornstalks scratched my face, and the layers of clothes I wore were heavy and hot. I had to keep them on, though—what few valuables we'd been able to hide were sewn into them. The adults whispered as we trudged along in the moonlight. "Are we going the right way?" "Are we close?"

Our guide signaled that we were near the border. Everyone held their breath. Suddenly, there was a loud cry.

"Stoi!"

In seconds, Russian soldiers surrounded us, shouting words I couldn't understand. *We've been captured!*

'Tis the human touch in this world that counts, the touch of your hand and mine, which means far more to the fainting heart than shelter and bread and wine.

SPENCER MICHAEL FREE

My nightmare had begun three years earlier. I was only eleven years old then, that cold winter morning in 1944 when the Russians invaded my hometown of Gakowa. "Everyone must assemble in the town square!" someone shouted, running down our street. "Leave your doors unlocked!"

Our small town was located in Yugoslavia, just three miles from the Hungarian border. Most of the families spoke German—we were descendents of German farmers who had settled here two hundred years before. We weren't Nazis, and we didn't want anything to do with Hitler or the Holocaust. But now that World War II was ending, the Russian army decided that we were "the enemy," all because we had German blood.

Kindness is gladdening the hearts of those who are traveling the dark journey with us.
HENRI-FREDERIC AMIEL

My mother grabbed my three-year-old sister, Erna, by the hand and led us to the center of town, where many of our neighbors were waiting. *I wish Papa were here*, I thought. Two months earlier, my father had been drafted into the German army.

Russian soldiers directed us to the town hall, where they searched us for money and valuables. Then, the Russian commander made an announcement: "Your homes are no longer your own.

Everything you have now belongs to Russia!" The guards forced us inside the houses closest to the town square. They locked the doors, leaving a guard in front.

There were so many women and children crammed inside the house that I could barely breathe. That night, my mother, my sister, and I found a small area on the floor to lie down. "What will happen to us tomorrow?" I asked Mother as she stroked Erna's hair.

"There are good people everywhere, Katherine. We'll be all right," she said. I held tight to her words as I fell asleep.

The only people with whom you should try to get even are those who have helped you.
John E. Southard

The next morning, some of the men and women were ordered to go and feed the livestock at all the homes in town. They came back with terrible news. The soldiers had robbed our homes, taking everything of value they could find—including some of the food we'd stored for winter. What they didn't want, they destroyed. Furniture was set on fire and clothes were torn and thrown into the street. We were forced to stay in our prison for two weeks, with only one outhouse, a well, and very little food. Then one day we were released to go back to our homes. *The worst must be over*, I thought.

But the horror was just beginning. Within a few weeks, many of our neighbors were sent to labor camps. The rest of us remained prisoners in our own homes. That spring, hundreds of people from other German-speaking towns were marched into Gakowa. They were forced to live in our houses with us. Our town soon became the most dreaded war camp in Yugoslavia.

There were so many people, and there was so little space. We slept in bedrooms with as many as twenty people, and we were constantly hungry. I was always covered in filth, since bathing was nearly impossible. Rats were everywhere. I dreaded falling asleep, knowing they'd crawl over me during the night.

Difficulties are meant to rouse, not discourage. The human spirit is to grow by conflict.

WILLIAM ELLERY CHANNING

If my mother was scared, she never showed it. She truly believed that God was watching over us, and that he would help us get through this. Her faith gave me hope. And her quiet strength made me stronger, too.

One day, as my mother and I watched a group of old people and children marching by, a man fell out of line. "Please, may I have a drink of water?" My mother ran to our well and brought back a cup.

"Thank you a thousand times, dear lady," he whispered before gulping it down. "We came from Apatin, where I just buried my wife. She died of typhoid fever."

He moved quickly back in line to avoid the soldiers' wrath. My mother waved to him, then walked back to the well to get more water. She took a sip, then gave some to me.

The ideas that have lighted my way have been kindness, beauty, and truth.
Albert Einstein

A week later, my mother and I were in bed with a terrible fever, a rash covering our bodies. "Typhoid," I heard someone whisper as I slipped in and out of consciousness. The disease was very contagious, so our house was evacuated. My sister was taken to the home of a relative, and a sign was posted on our door, warning of danger. Even the soldiers stayed away. Only my grandparents risked their lives to care for us.

Sometimes, I could hear my mother calling for me. "Katherine!" she would moan. But I couldn't respond.

The fever raged for twenty-one days. One day, I awoke to crying and wailing. "What's wrong?" I asked.

"Your mother has died, Katherine," my grandmother told me gently. I was so weak, I could barely comprehend it.

Finally, my fever subsided. I'd lost so much weight that I couldn't walk. When I looked in the mirror, I didn't recognize myself because my hair had fallen out. I sank to the floor, sobbing. I had nothing left. Nothing.

Not long after that, the soldiers took our house to use as their headquarters. My father had been gone for months and we feared he was dead. His parents took my sister Erna in, and I was sent to my aunt's house. "If the Russians find out your parents have died, they will take you away," my aunt told me. "So just say you are our daughter." I knew that orphans were sent to Serbia, where they were taught communism and raised to forget their families and their religion.

Flatter me, and I may not believe you. Criticize me, and I may not like you. Ignore me, and I may not forgive you. Encourage me, and I will not forget you.

WILLIAM ARTHUR WARD

I lived in constant fear. Once, Erna and I hid in a storage room for a week to avoid soldiers looking for orphans. Another time, we spent three days curled up in an old icebox in the tavern that our great-aunt owned. "Don't cry," I whispered to Erna, as we heard the sounds of soldiers raiding homes nearby. "If we're quiet they won't find us." And thankfully, they never did.

As the months passed, conditions in Gakowa got worse and worse. Soldiers called surprise "assemblies" at a moment's notice and sent the healthiest-looking people to labor camps. Other times they shot people dead in the street for no reason at all. Finally, it got so bad that my aunt and uncle made the desperate decision to attempt an escape. They'd take me with them, they said. Erna was staying with another aunt, and they would be escaping a few weeks later.

"Will I ever see Erna again?" I asked my aunt.

"You will," she reassured me. "You must believe that!"

The day I hugged Erna goodbye, we both cried.

We shall draw from the heart of suffering itself the means of inspiration and survival.

Sir Winston Churchill

Now, as we stood surrounded by Russian solders, I was thankful that Erna wasn't with us. *Dear God, please watch over us,* I prayed silently.

We were told to walk to the border station. Once inside the small building, the soldiers motioned for us to sit down. By this time, it was dawn. As the day progressed, each family was interrogated and searched for valuables. The guards took anything they wanted.

When it was our turn, we placed our bundles on a table. As the guard looked through them, I thought of my mother. I pictured her watching over me, protecting me. *Be strong and have faith, and God will stand by you,* I could almost hear her say. *There are good people everywhere. . . .* Finally, the guards motioned us to rejoin the group. They hadn't searched me! Our jewelry that we had hidden and then sewn into our clothes was safe.

Then the commander addressed us. "I am letting you go. . . ."

I could hardly believe my ears. *He's letting us go?*

Amazed, we gathered our bundles and continued our journey. No one could believe what had just happened. "Maybe the guards were tired of leading prisoners back to the camp," someone suggested. "Maybe they just wanted to get rid of us!"

But I knew the truth. It was a miracle. Here in the heat of hatred and inhumanity, that commander had spared our lives. *Be strong and have faith.* As we crossed the border into Hungary, I lifted my head and walked toward freedom.

Can I see another's woe, and not be in sorrow too? Can I see another's grief, and not seek for kind relief?
William Blake

Taking Flight

BY TARA BOICE

Life had become unbearable for me since my boyfriend and I had broken up a year ago. The smallest problem seemed insurmountable. Even eating became a chore, and I lost a lot of weight. I became so depressed that I left my apartment only to drag myself to work. So I was not thrilled about meeting Sarah for dinner one evening.

Love is patient, love is kind.
1 Corinthians 13:4

Sarah and I had been friends forever. I admired her enthusiasm for life, her way of meeting problems head-on. We had always been able to share our problems with each other—at least until the last few months, when I felt more and more isolated from everyone, including Sarah.

She had invited me to her house, which overlooked a small lake. As I pulled up, she opened the door, smiled, and told me she was looking forward to our time together.

An hour later, after a meal that I pushed away barely eaten, Sarah settled in her chair. "So what are you doing with your free time?" she asked.

"Not much," I shrugged.

She'd been getting these sad, limp answers from me all evening. "Tara," she said softly, "you're not going to feel better until you help someone or something less fortunate than yourself. Then you'll realize that things aren't as bad as you think."

I was silent, torn between anger at what I felt was her lack of sympathy and my own stirring that maybe, just maybe, she was right. I was so absorbed in my thoughts that for a few moments I didn't realize Sarah had slipped a book in front of me. It was the Bible.

She reached across the table and put her hand over mine. "I want you to have this. It's gotten me through some tough times in my life, and it can be something to hold onto in yours."

Don't judge each day by the harvest you reap, but by the seeds you plant.

Robert Louis Stevenson

For as long as I could remember, Sarah had attended church. Once, when I had marveled at the time she made in her busy schedule to attend services and study groups, she merely smiled and replied that it was no sacrifice at all. I found myself accepting the leather-bound volume she had handed me.

On the drive home, I thought about what she'd said. But the next day, I lapsed back into my old pattern of existence: dragging myself out of bed, skipping breakfast, barely making it to work on time, and coming home to a lonely night in front of the television. Weeks passed and the Bible lay unopened on my dresser.

Then one morning I got a telephone call. "Hello, this is Cathy from the Seabird Sanctuary," came a cheery voice.

Sarah, I thought. She had given my name as a posible volunteer to the Suncoast Seabird Sanctuary, a nonprofit organization that took care of and rehabilitated injured or sick wild birds. Cathy, one of the lab assistants there, was asking for my help in setting up an emergency hospital. An oil spill had occurred near Saint Petersburg, Florida, and the oil had already reached the shore at nearby Fort De Soto. The staff at the sanctuary were desperately concerned for the local wildlife, especially the seabirds.

If what must be given is given willingly the kindness is doubled.

Publilius Syrus

At first I was angry that Sarah had butted in. But I didn't have the heart to turn down the sanctuary.

So the next morning I was on the beach at a mobile hospital, up to my elbows in birds. A volunteer placed a bedraggled cormorant in front of me. He had been lifted out of a slimy pool among the rocks, and the tub for cleaning him was filled and ready. It's essential to clean an oil-saturated bird as soon as possible, before the bird has a chance to preen its feathers and swallow the toxic oil. As another volunteer helped me steady the scrawny, brown bird, I gently but firmly dunked him into the warm water.

Cathy walked over to inspect our efforts and gave a low whistle. "Boy, he's one-hundred-percent saturated, all right."

I knew there was little hope for a bird that was completely covered in oil. He had probably already eaten too much of it. But if this bird wouldn't give up, neither would I!

It took four of us working together to remove the oil. Two held the bird and one controlled the water temperature while I scrubbed off the sticky oil that clung to his delicate feathers. I gently swabbed the cormorant's eyes, then applied ointment to lubricate and protect them. His struggles ceased, as if he knew we were trying to help him. After what seemed an eternity, his brilliant turquoise eyes were clear, and he stared at us intently. I forced my hands to stop shaking as another of the volunteers handed me a syringe filled with a high-potency liquid diet. I squirted the liquid down his gullet, and followed it with a dose of Pepto-

To the world you might be one person, but to one person you might be the world.

Author Unknown

Bismol, to coat his stomach and prevent any more oil from being absorbed.

But it wasn't over yet. One washing hadn't removed all the oil. He needed to be transported to the sanctuary for additional treatment.

Birds are quite susceptible to chills, so I wrapped the cormorant in a thick towel and cradled him gently on my lap. I felt a sense of peace as I gazed at the wild animal, who looked back at me with such trust. I couldn't let this guy down. His survival was somehow linked with mine. He had given me a reason to fight. I had to trust too.

When we arrived at the sanctuary, another bath was prepared. The cormorant was scrubbed with dish detergent and warm water several more times. Finally, we placed the shivering bird in the hot box—a wooden container fitted with a warm-air blower—to protect him from hypothermia. If he could get through the night, his chances for survival were good. But he'd been through a lot. Would he make it?

Wise sayings often fall on barren ground; but a kind word is never thrown away.

Sir Arthur Helps

When I went home, I couldn't sleep. As I tossed and turned I was aware of the Bible on my dresser. For the first time since Sarah gave it to me, I opened it.

The words on the page I randomly opened to leaped out at me: "But they that wait upon the Lord shall renew their strength; they shall mount up with wings as eagles; they shall run, and not be weary; and they shall walk, and not faint" (Isaiah 40:31, KJV).

All through the night I read, sometimes aloud. And I prayed with a strength I hadn't felt in a long time. "Lord," I said, "please help that bird to survive. He deserves to live."

Early the next morning, I hurried to the sanctuary. I bolted through the door and raced to the hot box. I undid the latch, opened the door, and looked in. Two turquoise eyes looked back at me.

A candle loses nothing by lighting another candle.
Erin Majors

Six weeks later, on a warm and windy morning, we walked out to the beach to set him free. The cormorant had been given only a one-percent chance of survival. It had taken many long days of rehabilitation, but he was now well enough to be released.

I learned a lot from this feathered friend. I know that life is a precious gift from God, and I'm thankful for each day that is granted to me.

I watched the beautiful bird spread his wings and lift off into the sky. Through the kindness of others, he was whole again. And so was I.